The Interior Design

SOURCEBOOK

Thomas L. Williams

ALLWORTH PRESS

NEW YORK

Allworth Press books may be purchased in bulk at special discounts for sales promotion, corporate gifts, fund-raising, or educational purposes. Special editions can also be created to specifications. For details, contact the Special Sales Department, Allworth Press, 307 West 36th Street, 11th Floor, New York, N.Y. 10018 or info@skyhorsepublishing.com.

15 14 13 12 11   5 4 3 2 1

Published by Allworth Press
an imprint of Skyhorse Publishing, Inc.
307 West 36th Street, 11th Floor, New York, N.Y. 10018.

Allworth Press® is a registered trademark of Skyhorse Publishing, Inc.®, a Delaware corporation.

www.allworth.com

ISBN: 978-1-58115-898-4

Library of Congress Cataloging-in-Publication Data is available on file.

Printed in China

CONTENTS

Introduction   *1*

Part 1—Timeless and Enduring: Classic   7

Part 2—Updated and Durable: Contemporary   79

Part 3—Exciting and Sustainable: Modern   151

Afterword   *201*

Resources   *205*

Index   *223*

INTRODUCTION

With its wealth of natural resources, our planet has been the repository of all we use in our daily lives, both for sustenance and shelter, since long before recorded time. Stone, wood, and metal ores were among the first items manipulated by man, and our ability to mold these items to our needs continues to this day. With the advent of farming and herding, we learned how to use fibers and fabrics for our comfort and adornment. During the Renaissance, we learned to fashion natural elements into astounding displays of architectural and aesthetic beauty. Artisans, builders, and craftsmen envisioned and created works of art in every genre to please the eye, satisfy the soul, and surround us in comfort.

Since man combined tin and copper to create bronze, he has continued to look for ways to produce new and durable metals. By the early 18th century, with the advent of the industrial revolution, man began to manipulate elements in previously unthought-of ways. By the late 19th and early 20th centuries, the development of strong structural metals helped create the cityscapes we know today and the buildings in which most of us live. Since the middle of the 18th century, furniture makers, upholsterers, and sundry craftsmen have endeavored to procure and manipulate a wealth of natural and man-made resources when producing interiors for clients far and wide.

Today's interior design professionals have at their command a plethora of materials, fabrics, colors, items, and tools to produce some of the most beautiful and creative interiors in the world. With this breadth of choice comes an overwhelming array of elements, items, and possibilities. Understanding the resources with which we work is part and parcel of our job as professional interior designers. It is up to us to understand which element is the correct choice for a particular application and explain to our

clientele why it is so. As professionals we need to understand how a product or element is grown, manufactured, or produced to have a clear idea of how best to use it in any given installation.

The Interior Design Sourcebook is designed to help you and your client understand what an element is and how it might be used in today's modern interior designs. From classic and traditional materials to the most cutting-edge, sustainable, and ecofriendly ones, this book will define the elements of interior design, discuss their applications and uses, and direct you to the best possible resources to find everything needed to complete a refined and elegant interior.

Starting with classic elements like stone, wood, fibers, and metals, *The Interior Design Sourcebook* considers new uses and applications for traditional materials. Durable and reassuring,

these elements have nonetheless been manipulated to be even more enduring and usable. Professional interior designers need to understand the changes and adaptations that have been made to best utilize these elements.

Contemporary elements encompass those used first in industrial or commercial applications before finding their way, in the late 19th and early 20th centuries, into residential use. It was during this period that concrete, steel, and structural elements began to play a larger part in interior

design, and understanding how to use these elements in less-rigid residential interiors without giving up their inherent noble characteristics is part of understanding how they are made and used today.

Professional interior design has experienced explosive growth since the end of World War II, and the use of both classic and contemporary elements has created the modern interiors we currently enjoy. Modern elements are a combination of classic sensibilities and an out-of-the-box approach to application and function. Fabrics that change with the light and concrete that is almost transparent create a sense of drama and excitement while allowing modern interiors to remain warm and inviting.

As we have become more attuned to our needs and the needs of the planet as a whole, we've learned to appreciate and embrace reclaimed and recycled elements. Many of these elements, too, have come from commercial and industrial areas into our homes, and understanding their origins will help when deciding what application is best for you and your client. The reclamation of elements and the use of secondhand materials has become one of the standard tools of our trade, and sustainability has come to the fore as one of the most important aspects of material

acquisition and use. Our understanding of how an element is created helps us make thoughtful and sensitive decisions about its use within modern interior design installations.

Appropriate choices made in an efficient and thoughtful manner will help any professional interior designer satisfy his or her clientele and, at the same time, create sumptuous and refined interiors. A clear and complete understanding of resources and acquisition will help make any designer's job easier and more rewarding. *The Interior Design Sourcebook* provides the tools necessary to meet client obligations, satisfy aesthetic parameters, meet ecological considerations, and produce interiors that will provide functional and comfortable surroundings.

PART ONE

TIMELESS AND ENDURING: CLASSIC

Classic materials are those with which we have a long and productive history. Elements such as wood, stone, and fabric have long been used to great advantage in interior design and continue to this day to provide warmth, reassurance, and a quiet sense of serenity. In short, these elements are the foundation on which most interior designers base their projects. We are comfortable with these elements because we know them so well. We know how to use them to our best advantage; we are comfortable with installation and application; we understand their characteristics. Most of us grew up with the warm, rich glow of beautifully polished wood finishes and the intricate and interesting way in which the grain of wood plays with the curve of a chair leg or headboard. We understand the cool, elegant appeal of marble and stone,

which enhance the beauty of other elements in a room. Classic elements provide a sense of security and permanence. Are they, therefore, too restrained and conservative to be actually usable in today's interiors? Of course not.

The essence of appropriate application is in the new and exciting ways in which classic elements are used today. Wood is combined with glues and high heat to produce strong and durable beams for construction as well as light and easily manipulated panels for furniture and paneling. Marble has come up from the floor and is used on walls and even ceilings as an expression of a more updated aesthetic. These elements are as vital a part of the whole as when they were first used centuries ago.

The true building blocks of design, these elements are easily sourced and installed. We all

have a very clear understanding of how they are manufactured and used in both traditional and modern interiors. Each is highly adaptable to the needs of the professional interior designer and the requirements of residential interior installations.

STONE

The oldest of all the elements on Earth, stone is the epitome of durability and permanence. Stone can impart a refined and elegant look or a downright rustic appeal. Which stone is selected and how it is finished defines its ultimate expression. From heroic, columned Federal buildings to sleek, refined contemporary inte-

riors, stone always conveys a sense of power and permanence.

As a dense material, stone is slow to gather heat and slow to release it. This particular attribute makes stone a wonderful choice for spaces designed with passive solar heating in mind, as well as spaces using underfloor heating systems. Stone is used in construction in areas of the world that experience hot summers and cool or cold winters because of its ability to retain and release heat slowly.

Although exceptionally hard and unyielding, stone is not completely solid. Even granite must be sealed after installation to help prevent stains

and spots associated with use. Stone is also very heavy, and it requires expert installation to ensure that cracks don't appear under floors and on countertops. Extra support must always be used when installing flooring or counters to support the additional weight stone brings to any use. The precise fabrication techniques used and the expert installation required add to the cost of stone. It still remains, however, the first choice of many clients and professional interior designers for floors, countertops, and bath-rooms. As you will see, various types of stone lend themselves to applications and uses not found with some other types of materials.

Just the Facts

Stone comes in many forms and is found in every part of the world. There are three main types of stone, each reflective of how the stone was deposited when formed. Igneous rock, which is formed through the cooling and solidi-fication of magma or lava, also known as molten

rock, is the oldest of all stones. The most commonly used igneous rock in interior design is granite, which comes in a variety of shades and colors to suit most design palettes.

Metamorphic rocks, found in mountainous areas, are deposited when mountain ranges are formed; they are the by-products of intense heat and pressure from those formations. Slate and marble are fine examples of metamorphic rocks.

The third type of stone is called sedimentary. These rocks, such as limestone and sandstone,

are formed by deposits on lake, sea, and river bottoms. The weight of additional deposits compacts the lower levels and creates these softer stones. Softer than both granite and marble, sedimentary stone requires extra expertise during installation and finishing to ensure superior performance.

If possible, find a local stone appropriate to your application. It will cost less to transport and should also reflect a more local approach to your interior expression. You should also consider

reclaimed stone if possible. Salvage and architectural yards offer the best choices for this type of stone.

Granite

The use of granite in residential interiors has become a staple of professional interior designers. This very dense, hard, and smooth stone is one of the most resilient materials used in residential design today. It can be honed to a beautiful smooth finish and has a wide selection of colors and shades to enhance any interior. Its unique appearance is unforgettable and not easily replicated by any other material. Depending on where the granite is quarried, it can contain mineral feldspar, mica, and deposits of quartz, which create the coloring and shading inherent to that particular type of granite. Found all over the world, granite is a particularly diverse material suitable for many types of interior design. Mixed with other elements, such as wood or metal, the possibilities are limitless.

QUALITIES

Granite is hard, dense, and heavy. It is extraordinarily resistant and will last for years with little or no sign of use. The color spread is consistent, with an even, flecked pattern and a small, grainy texture. Thin slabs and tiles crack and break easily. Granite is available in large, solid slabs as well as thinner, lighter tiles and pavers.

HOW IT'S USED

Granite is a practical choice for kitchen counters, bar tops, and vanities in bathrooms. Backsplash and edging details offer great finish options. Tiles can be used for fireplace surrounds and built-in bathroom fixtures such as tubs and showers. Tiles for flooring in both kitchen and bath can be honed for reduced slipping.

FINISHING

Polished to a high gloss, granite shows its natural beauty in both color and markings.

Granite should be sealed after installation to improve ease of maintenance.

Marble

From Michelangelo's *David* in Florence, Italy, to the row-house stoops in Baltimore, Maryland's, neighborhoods, marble has always been the first choice of artists and designers as an expression of the ultimate in luxury and sophistication. With a deep, almost translucent quality provided by impurities in the stone, marble has a certain warmth and an inviting quality many

other stones lack. Subtle cracks, veining, and fissures add to marble's unique accessibility and popularity. Carrara, Italy, produces the finest and whitest marble on earth. Sculptors prize this marble above all others. The Carrara quarries still operate today, and their marble is shipped all over the world.

QUALITIES

Marble is a heavy, dense stone. It can be polished to a highly reflective finish and is available in a wide range of colors and shades. Pink, dull gold, and green vie with white as the most popular colors used. Less impervious to staining than granite, marble must be sealed to ensure stain resistance and ease of maintenance. The expense has come down due to new cutting methods. Lighter, thinner tiles and slabs are more prone to cracking and breaking.

HOW IT'S USED

Marble has been used for years in both public and private bathrooms. Once sealed, it is relatively easy to maintain. It is suitable for flooring in entryways and other areas. Edge profiles are also available. It can be

used in surrounds for fireplaces and for mantels.

FINISHING

Honed, marble is less slippery than polished tiles. Tumbled marble has also become very popular. The tumbling process softens the sharp edges and creates a more rustic finish. This also makes the surface less slippery.

Slate

From beautiful slate roofs to patio paving, slate is a versatile and easily worked element. A metamorphic rock created from shale by centuries of pressure, it can be cut easily and split to create thin layers of usable stone. Slate can be found in parts of Africa, Europe, South America, and North America.

QUALITIES

Slate is hard, waterproof, and long wearing. It is easily split into thin planes and is laterally strong, resulting in tiles not easily broken while in use. Due to the amount of mica present, slate has a deep, almost wet look. It is available in darker colors: black, green, purple, and gray-green. Slates from different parts of the world offer variety in color and texture.

HOW IT'S USED

Slate is used in flooring, tiling, roofing, cladding, shelving, and counter-tops.

FINISHING

Slate must be sealed before and after grouting.

Travertine

Travertine is a sedimentary stone formed by layers of calcite deposited by organic matter in hot springs and spas. Fossilized traces of leaves, feathers, and branches are often found in travertine stone. For centuries, travertine has been prized for its beauty and hardness as a construction material. One of the most famous sources is Tivoli, outside of Rome; this travertine was used to clad the Colosseum.

QUALITIES

Travertine's honeycomb structure is the result of water bubbling up through the deposits prior to crystallization; this results in small holes and pits on the surface of the cut stone. It is very strong, despite its pitted appearance. Pure travertine is white. Colors, from gray to coral red, result from the presence of mineral impurities. It is available in slabs, tiles, and cladding panels.

HOW IT'S USED

Travertine is often used as a facade for buildings. Both tiles and slabs can be used for flooring indoors and out. Panels can be used for cladding walls.

FINISHING

Honed surfaces are the best choice for travertine. Holes on the surface can be left unfilled for a rustic, natural appearance or filled at the factory or on-site with hard resins and honed smooth. Travertine requires sealing to prevent stains and dirt from collecting in crevices.

Limestone

Like other sedimentary rocks, limestone is composed of minute granules of calcium, which

is the residue of organic matter like shellfish, coral, and plants deposited in rivers and oceans. As the layers thicken, pressure increases, and over millions of years, limestone is formed. Limestone is more porous and softer than igneous rock but can approach the hardness of granite.

Limestone is quarried in many parts of the world, and in America, Indiana limestone is prized for its color and hardness. French limestone is also prized for its consistent hardness; it is less porous than many other limestones. Limestone is also used to clad the exterior of buildings and gives a milky-white depth of color when used in large expanses over walls.

QUALITIES

The color of limestone ranges from the pale white mentioned above to a bright blue (very unusual in stone) with most of the shadings falling within the pale-beige to pale-gold color range. Gray is also a readily available color for limestone. Quite often the stone is filled with the fossilized remains of animal or vegetable life, and veins and mottling are desirable attributes of many limestone slabs. Limestone is available in slabs, tiles, and panels (for walls). It also works well as a tumbled tile to soften edges.

HOW IT'S USED

Limestone makes a wonderful and serviceable floor material when sealed properly. As a countertop, limestone needs extra care and might stain due to its porous nature.

FINISHING

Limestone quickly loses any high polish applied, so honing is the best approach for finishing. The matte surface created by sandblasting or honing makes the limestone less slippery and intensifies the shade of color in the stone. To protect the surface, limestone must be sealed after finishing. The sealing process must be repeated occasionally to prevent stains.

Sandstone

Sandstone is composed of millions of sand grains mixed with a high quartz content compacted over millions of years to form a very dense stone much harder than limestone. Sandstone is popular as outdoor paving material for patios and walkways and has been used as cladding on buildings for centuries.

QUALITIES

Sandstone is much harder and denser than most sedimentary stone. Its color ranges from sandy beige to almost reddish brown, with a granular texture derived from the sand composition. It is available in stepstones, tiles, and small blocks.

HOW IT'S USED

Sandstone is used mainly for flooring in today's interiors. It is also popular as an outdoor paving surface.

FINISHING

Sandstone must be sealed for indoor applications. When sandblasted or honed, sandstone offers good traction and nonslip properties.

Engineered Stone

A newer man-made product, engineered stone is more cost-effective than most other natural stone choices. Engineered stone is composed of a large percentage of natural stone, often quartz, combined with a mixture of resins, glues, and color to form a hard and serviceable product. In some engineered stones, the natural stone constitutes as much as 93 percent of the product. Engineered stones are generally maintenance-free, antibacterial, stain resistant, nonporous, and consistent in color and finish.

The product is easy to manufacture and install and can be used for countertops, shower enclosures, and backsplashes. With a wide range of color, manufactured stone is versatile and offers designers choices not often found with natural stone.

Function, Style, and Maintenance

Stone is a natural material, and there will always be shading, color, and pitting variances, even within stone from the same quarry. When selecting slabs, it is best to visit a reputable stone yard and actually view all selected slabs side by side to determine whether or not they will work together to create a balanced and consistent finished product. When working with tiles and smaller pieces of material, it is advisable to actually set out a large portion of the tiles to view how they will flow from one to the other. Once everyone is happy with the result, an installer can lay the tiles.

WASTE

Like many other products we use for interiors, there will be a proportion of a slab or group of tiles that will be waste. Countertops will never be exactly the shape and size of the

slab, and tiles need to be cut to fit properly in any installation. Reputable slab masons understand what is needed and will advise as to how large each slab should be for a complete installation. The same applies to tiles, but a general rule of thumb is to allow between 10 and 15 percent for overage. For both slabs and tiles it is possible for breakage or cracking to occur during shipping, so overage is part of the cost of the installation.

FLOORS

Tiles and, to a small extent, slabs work beautifully for flooring when installed properly.

Patterns can be created depending on what you find pleasing, and a mix of color and pattern often adds interest and excitement where before there was none. It is important to work with a professional interior designer to create the correct scale and proportion for any installation with a pattern.

Subflooring and preparation for installation are important. The base must be even, stable, perfectly flat, and able to withstand the extra weight of the stone. In many instances, an engineer might need to be consulted to ensure that the structure will bear the additional load of a room full of stone. Second floor applications are particular vulnerable, and structures should always be reviewed before installation.

Tiles are set in place using an adhesive, and the small spaces between are filled with sand or a sand-and-cement grout combination. Usually, the grout is very close in color to the tile, but on occasion, a designer might choose a contrasting grout.

Even, regularly shaped tiles are often placed very close to one another, while tumbled or handmade tiles require more room.

Once in place, the floor is sealed with products designed specifically for each type of installation.

Most stone installations require some small space around the perimeter for expansion and contraction. Heat and cold will work on a large expanse of stone, and there will always be slight movement.

WALLS

Wall tiles are very thin compared to floor tiles and are adhered to the wall prior to finishing with grout. These applications, too, must be sealed once the grout is dry.

COUNTERTOPS, WORK SURFACES, HEARTHS, AND FIRE SURROUNDS

Stone slabs, usually ranging from one to two inches in thickness, are the material of choice for most countertops and work surfaces. Their clean, open look works beautifully with the expanse of most kitchen counters. Large slabs help keep cuts and seams to a minimum. Installation, like flooring, requires a stable and secure base on which the slab will rest. It is also important to ensure that the cabinets and flooring can accommodate the extra weight of stone slabs. Edge finishes and backsplashes are all made from the waste cut out of the major slab and are adhered by gluing in place.

MAINTENANCE

Stone is not indestructible, and routine maintenance is necessary to ensure quality performance with each installation. To prevent dirt buildup and accumulation of grime, all stone should be sealed upon installation and allowed to set before using. The sealant should also be refreshed from time to time. Tile stone should also be sealed before and after grouting to prevent staining during the grout process.

Counters should be cleaned with a neutral cleanser or mild washing liquid. Avoid using too much detergent, and be sure to remove all soap film with clear, clean water.

Acids, such as lemon, cola, wine, and vinegar, are particularly destructive to stone finishes and should be wiped up immediately.

Do not use oils or wax polishes on surfaces.

Floors require many of the same maintenance procedures and will also need to be cleaned with a dry dust mop. Flooring is prone to grit, which is most damaging on stone surfaces, so be sure to place mats at doorways and entrances to prevent dust and grit from being tracked all over the stone floor. Avoid wet mopping. As with countertops, avoid oils and wax cleaners on flooring.

BRICK AND CERAMIC

Take a little earth, add some straw, form into a rectangular mold, and let it bake in the sun. Bricks and, to a certain extent tiles, are made of the simplest of ingredients and are easy to form and hold. Generally scaled to the size of the human hand, bricks have been used for construction since before Egyptian times and continue to be used today. Brick and other ceramic products have an almost mesmerizing allure due to the

rhythmic patterns created when they are installed. They are both warm and sophisticated in the truest sense of the words.

Brick isn't as massive and robust as stone, but it possesses some of stone's best attributes. Brick is dense and holds and releases heat very slowly. Have you ever stood next to a west-facing brick wall at dusk? The warmth radiating out from the wall is both comforting and homey. Brick is part of our very souls and has been used by every segment of the population for eons.

As humans discovered that cities built of wood burn readily, they turned to brick as a material with which to clad buildings and help make them less prone to the ravages of fire.

Relatively inexpensive and easy to install, brick became the defining element of domestic construction in many Northern European and North American cities in the early 18th century. Vast sections of London and New York City are etched in our minds with the color and pattern of brick facades.

Ceramic tiles are earthen tiles made from refined clay, glazed in wonderful colors, and fired to create the hard, bright finishes we all know. Terra-cotta tiles, which were the precursor to ceramic tiles, are also handmade but allowed to remain in an unglazed and unpainted state on firing. Ubiquitous in Southern Europe, Northern Africa, and Mexico, handmade terra-cotta tiles are simple to produce and easy to apply. They

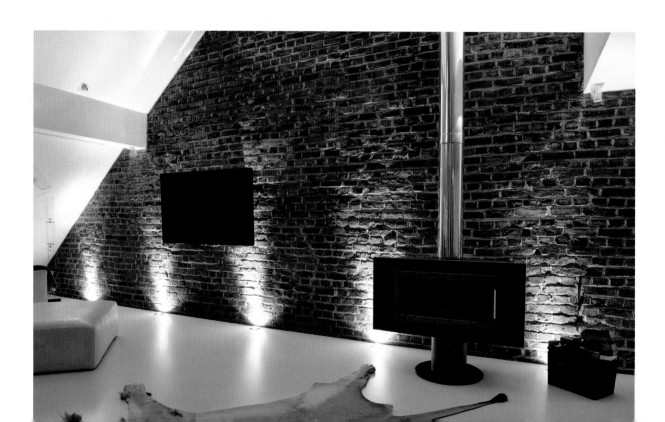

also helped define Spanish Colonial architecture at home and in the New World.

Ceramic and terra-cotta tiles are perfect choices for kitchens and bathrooms. They are waterproof, easy to clean, and hard wearing. The patterns for ceramic tiles are endless; they can be combined in hundreds of ways to create pattern and rhythm for ultrachic loft apartments or rustic farmhouses. Today, most ceramic and terra-cotta tiles are machine-made, but there is a growing trend towards handmade tiles for a bespoke aesthetic in some interior installations.

Along with ceramics, the art of mosaic installation has returned to prominence in the past few decades. Using numerous smaller pieces of tile, mosaics can create wonderful patterns and even scenic displays depending on how they are assembled.

Just the Facts

Brick and ceramic tend to be inexpensive and are easy to use and install. Almost anyone can learn to install both brick wall and ceramic flooring. In flooring, large tiles work best in grander, more open spaces. Smaller tiles are more suited to the powder room and smaller areas of the home. Both benefit from grand use of materials. A small row of tile or a tiny section of floor doesn't show these elements to their best advantage. Broad sweeps of tile, full walls of ceramic, and large buildings of brick are far more expressive of the fundamental power of the humble brick and ceramic tile.

Brick

Before the 19th century, all brick was hand-made by local artisans. Each area had its own style and color of brick. Even then, however, most bricks were about the same size, no matter where they were made. As you can imagine, brick buildings from area to area varied greatly in color and appearance. With the advent of the industrial age and large factories, brick quickly became standardized and dependable. Brick remains today very much as it was in the past. Almost all bricks fit comfortably in the hand of the mason, and all are generally the same weight.

TYPES OF BRICK

Standard Construction Bricks

As the name implies, all the same size, color, weight, and density.

Weathered Brick

Sometimes referred to as used brick, weathered brick is tumbled to give it a softer, worn-look. Not to be confused with true reclaimed brick.

Lightweight Bricks

To create greater insulation properties, these bricks are honeycombed with tiny air pockets before being fired.

Wire-Cut Brick

This brick is an extruded product, which is then cut into bricks for a very crisp, straight edge.

Brick Pavers

These bricks are thinner than most and are used for applications on walls and as flooring. These bricks are durable, waterproof inherently slip resistant, and easy to maintain.

QUALITIES

Generally, brick should be laid by a professional. Brick is easily stained and slightly porous.

Weight is a factor when using brick, and structural integrity is important before selecting brick as a facade material. Brick is warm in color and texture and lends itself to a wide variety of patterns such as herringbone and basket weave.

HOW IT'S USED

Brick is used in masonry construction to form load-bearing walls. It is used for internal walls and partitions, fireplace surrounds, and flooring. Exposed brick makes a warm and cozy backdrop for many modern interiors. Outdoor applications, such as paving, should use only vitrified bricks.

FINISHING

Generally, sealing is not advised for brick installation. Interior brick walls should be dusted occasionally. Brick is, as a rule, maintenance-free. Should efflorescence (deposits of white mineral salts) appear, simply wash with warm water. To increase the color possibilities, brick can be painted and will still retain its inherent rhythm and pattern.

Terra-Cotta Tiles

Like brick, terra-cotta tiles started as hand-made elements made from local clay and earth in many parts of the world. These tiles can be glazed or unglazed and come in a wide variety of colors and shading due to differences in earth and clay. Most, however, have distinct shading in the red or ocher range. The irregularities inherent in terra-cotta tiles produced by the handmade process give them great character and vitality. Machine-made tiles are more uniform yet retain the colorful and rustic feel of handmade tiles.

TYPES OF TERRA-COTTA TILES

Unglazed Handmade Tiles

Artisan-made tiles are readily available throughout North America. Many, of course, are produced in Mexico in the traditional manner. Earth and clay are mixed together and shaped by hand. They are baked in the sun and then transferred to a kiln for final firing, glazed or unglazed. Paler shades, ranging from pinks to light yellow, can be found in southern France, with deep red and ocher tiles coming from northern Italy. Mexico produces lively orange colors with vibrant shadings for a deep, inviting finish.

Unglazed Machine-Made Tiles

Machine-made tiles have a finer surface finish and are more regular in shape than hand-made tiles. Computer techniques are employed to produce varieties very similar to handmade, which can be distressed or even tumbled to create softer edges and seams.

Glazed Tiles

Both handmade and machine-made tiles come in a variety of colors and patterns for any interior design installation. All areas produce exuberant patterns and lavish finishes on glazed tiles.

Reclaimed Tiles

Found in old farmhouses, barns, and courtyards, old tiles have become popular in the interior design business. These tiles are difficult to collect and are very pricey.

QUALITIES

With age, the patina of terra-cotta deepens and becomes almost leathery in appearance. It is very durable; glazed tiles are not as resilient as unglazed tiles. Like brick, these tiles absorb and release heat very slowly. Although generally square in appearance, terra-cotta tiles come in a variety of shapes and sizes.

HOW THEY'RE USED

Unglazed terra-cotta tiles are used exclusively for floors and should be installed by a competent professional due to the variations of thickness and edges on almost all tiles. Weight is a factor, and these tiles must be laid over a subfloor that is dry, even, and stable. Tiles are set directly in cement or mortar or glued down, then finished with grout.

Glazed tiles are not durable enough to be used on the floor but make delightful and interesting vertical features for walls, backsplashes, and stair risers.

FINISHING

Some tiles are sealed by the manufacturer, but most require an application of linseed oil due to the porous nature of the tiles. Tiles should be swept at regular intervals to prevent grit and dirt from damaging the surface. Even glazed tiles

are susceptible to stains, and the use of acidic liquids or strong detergents should be avoided.

Quarry Tiles

Quarry tiles are a cheap, factory-made alternative to terra-cotta tiles. They are made from clay with high silica content and are very utilitarian. Like terra-cotta tiles, quarry tiles are pressed into a form, then fired for strength and durability.

QUALITIES

Quarry tiles are cheap and rather static and lifeless when compared to terra-cotta tiles. They do not change color or texture with use.

Like all other earthen elements, quarry tiles absorb and lose heat slowly and are a good choice for installation over in-floor heating elements. Quarry tiles have a rather rough texture, are generally square in shape, and come in a limited range of colors—mostly earth tones of brown, beige, red, biscuit, and black.

They should be swept regularly to prevent scratches and gouges.

HOW THEY'RE USED

Quarry tiles are used almost exclusively as flooring. They are particularly good for high traffic areas, such as entries, kitchens, gardens, sunrooms, and utility rooms.

Finishing

Quarry tiles usually require nothing more than an occasional application of linseed oil or a light wax finish.

Ceramic Tiles

Ceramic tiles are divided into two types: nonporcelain and porcelain. Both are available in a huge range of patterns, shapes, sizes, and

colors, and both are very durable. Porcelain tiles, however, are stronger and more durable than nonporcelain tiles. Both nonporcelain and porcelain ceramic tiles are made from clay and fired in a kiln. Along with other minerals, feldspar contributes to the hardness of porcelain tiles, which are fired at a higher temperature than nonporcelain tiles.

Although ceramic tiles can be unglazed, the vast majority are glazed, and in some the color even goes right through the tile.

QUALITIES

Ceramic tiles are regular in size and depth and can easily be laid in tight grids with narrow grout lines. Rectangular "subway" glazed tiles have an early 20th-century feel and were used liberally in the New York City subway system in the 1920s and 1930s.

All ceramic tiles are durable, and porcelain tiles are almost 30 percent harder than granite. These tiles are less likely to chip or break than terra-cotta or even quarry tiles.

Although widely available, some of the most expensive ceramic tiles come from Italy and other parts of Europe. Porcelain ceramic tiles are more expensive than nonporcelain ceramic tiles.

Most ceramic tiles come with accessory beadings, trims, and other matching fitted pieces. They are available in a wide range of colors and patterns and are used in almost any style of interior design project, from traditional farmhouse to ultrachic, modern penthouse.

The drawbacks are that ceramic tiles can be cold underfoot and slippery when wet.

HOW THEY'RE USED

As with other tile projects, it is best to employ the services of a professional for the installation of ceramic tiles. There is waste involved due to shipping and the demands of the pattern, so plan on ordering at least 10 percent more than the actual square footage.

Some tiles are harder than others and should be chosen for floors that experience high traffic or heavy dirt and grit. Installation is much the same as that of other tiles, and a strong, solid subfloor is necessary to ensure good performance over the life of the floor.

The application of wall tiles, particularly in kitchens and bathrooms, can be highly successful if used lavishly. Many bathrooms have been tiled from floor to ceiling to great advantage. Should you stop the tiles lower than the ceiling, align the upper edge with the bottom or top of a window or other prominent feature. For installations in water areas, like around sinks or in tubs or showers, use a dependable waterproof adhesive over waterproof plasterboard.

Tiles used on horizontal surfaces like countertops and vanities are slightly thicker than tiles used in vertical applications and should be stain and water-resistant. These tiles should also be fully vitrified to withstand heat.

FINISHING

Glazed ceramic tiles need no other finishing. All should be occasionally washed with a damp cloth. When grout becomes stained or discolored, clean with a stiff brush and a mild detergent.

Mosaic

Mosaic is the smallest tile used in interiors and is very effective in applications similar to those in which larger tiles are used. Mosaic is applied in a manner similar to other tiles but comes in glass as well as composite form rather than only earthen. The art is centuries old, and beautiful examples can be found all over the world. The Greeks and Romans used mosaic on walls as well as floors in almost all of their buildings, both private and public.

A pattern is made by using very small pieces of tile to create precise patterns or images as well as sweeping expanses of color and texture. Mosaic is particularly useful for kitchen back-splashes, bath and shower enclosures, fireplace surrounds, entry floors, and other spaces requiring texture and color.

QUALITIES

The allure of mosaic is its ability to project two very different effects, depending on whether you see it close up or step away to view the overall effect. The crispness of the tiles and intricacy of the color are what is appreciated up close, while the overall pattern and texture are what one experiences when standing back from the installation.

As with other tile forms, mosaic comes in a wide range of colors, styles, and textures. It is available as ceramic tile, glass tile, and stone tile. Glass and ceramic mosaic tiles are evenly sized and finished; they are easier to install than stone mosaic. Most mosaic today comes in sheet form, in which a net or paper backing is used to set the pattern. The installer simply lays the sheet as if it

were a single tile, then removes the backing to continue the installation.

The choice of grout helps define the ultimate effect of the mosaic. Whether using lighter grout with darker tiles or vice versa, the designer has a wealth of possibilities from which to choose.

HOW IT'S USED

For flooring, the requirements for mosaic are the same as other tile installations. Honed or tumbled stone mosaics are the best choices for flooring. Glass and ceramic won't perform as well in this particular application. Mosaic lends itself to walls with gentle curves, and when applied properly, it creates texture and movement in these areas. Depending on your taste and pocketbook, the possibilities are limitless. Mosaic can be created by artisan masons and can take weeks or even months to finish. The result, however—a unique and timeless installation—can be without peer and well worth the time and expense .

FINISHING

Washing with a mild detergent is usually sufficient to keep mosaic clean. Mosaic should never be polished with wax or other cleaning agents.

LINOLEUM

Linoleum is not an element that leaps quickly to the mind of most interior designers. It is, however, a durable and natural product, that is versatile, colorful, and chock-full of possibility. Developed in 1863 by Frederick Walton, linoleum is composed of linseed oil, jute (for backing), pine resin, powdered cork, wood flour, powdered limestone, and pigment (for color). After pressing the mixture onto the backing, it is left to dry for a few weeks, then baked at a high temperature to create the final result. Until about thirty years ago, linoleum was cheap, ugly, brittle, and best remembered in kitchens, hospitals, and

government hallways. Today, new techniques in manufacturing and the addition of bright colors and patterns have taken linoleum into some of the most exciting and interesting interiors in the country. The material is now far less prone to cracking, and this malleability allows for more intricate installations in pattern and color.

QUALITIES

Linoleum has a smooth finish with a mottled or granular appearance and is available in both sheet and tile form. Good-quality linoleum is strong, flexible, and thick. A shapeshifter of sorts, linoleum can contribute to a midcentury interior and in the next moment create an inviting and formal-feeling entry.

The texture can be changed depending on the content and mix of the material used in the creation of the product, and it is usually warm with a slight resilient feeling. Generally, there is a mottled or grainy appearance, and the colors available range from muted earth tones to vibrant and exciting solid primary colors.

Although water-resistant, linoleum can be damaged if water seeps between the joints and soaks into the subflooring. Linoleum is also burnresistant, antistatic, and hypoallergenic. Its antibacterial qualities still make it the first choice of many hospitals, clinics, schools, and other areas where hygiene plays a part in the decision as to which flooring to use.

Linoleum actually becomes harder and more resilient with age.

HOW IT'S USED

Linoleum is commonly used as flooring. Although still used primarily in kitchens, bath-rooms, and playrooms, its new incarnation, featuring new colors and patterns, also makes it a perfect choice for elegant living spaces when a glossy, stylish finish is desired.

A smooth and stable subfloor is necessary for linoleum to perform at its best; no small imperfection or ridge can remain.Place the product in the area in which it will be installed forty-eight hours before installation, as it must acclimat to the temperature and humidity of the space.

Tiles are the easiest to install; even an amateur can successfully lay linoleum flooring. Adhesive is applied, and the tiles are placed in the pattern desired. Individual tiles can be removed or replaced as needed with very little problem.

Sheet linoleum is heavier to manage due to the bulk of the roll, and a professional should be hired to install it correctly. A professional will also be able to heat-set the seams and ensure that the product is perfectly flat after installation.

Patterns can be achieved simply by alternating the color of tiles used into a checkerboard pattern, herringbone pattern, or any other type desired. The look of an area rug can be created by laying one color tile along the perimeter of the space and centering a second color in the middle. Linoleum can also be cut to create a mosaic effect. The use of a sharp and clean blade will ensure even edges for intricate pattern work. There are professional installers who have mastered the art of linoleum mosaic to create fanciful and creative floors.

FINISHING

Linoleum does not require any sort of sealing. If a glossy sheen is desired, a light water-based polish can be used. Don't overpolish as it

will create a slippery finish if even a small amount of moisture is present. Maintenance requires a light dust with a dry mop or the use of a vacuum cleaner. A mild detergent dissolved in water can also be used. Care should be taken to not allow water to seep into the seams. Although it is resistant to many chemicals, some solvents, oven cleaner, and washing soda can mar the finish on linoleum. Because the color in linoleum goes all the way through the material, light mars and burns can easily be rubbed away with little effect on the finish of the product.

Vinyl

Vinyl is a synthetic thermoplastic, developed in the early 1950s, whose basic ingredient is polyvinylchloride, or PVC. Although used primarily in the home as a flooring material,

PVC becomes soft and pliable when heated and can be molded into many different shapes for a myriad of uses.

Although the use of vinyl is discouraged by the green lobby, it is a durable flooring product that lasts for several decades and should not be looked upon as a disposable product.

Like linoleum, vinyl floor coverings are utilitarian and are most often seen in kitchens, laundry rooms, bathrooms, and utility rooms. The final product, the backing of which determines durability, is available in both tile and roll form and is composed of the backing, a printed layer for design and texture, and a clear film, that protects the vinyl from scratches and scuffs.

QUALITIES

Easily dyed, vinyl comes in a wide variety of colors, styles, and textures. Printing and embossing techniques allow designers to choose anything from simple, solid-colored tiles to product that mimics the look of wood flooring, stone, and ceramic tile. Vinyl with thicker backing is superior to lesser brands; it is more durable, water-resistant, and has the added benefit of softness underfoot.

Compared to most natural materials, vinyl is very cost-effective.

Vinyl is a product that produces "off-gas," particularly when new, and it can produce toxic fumes if it catches fire. As a petroleum product, it is not biodegradable, and care must be taken when disposing of or removing vinyl flooring from interior projects. Unlike stone and other natural products, vinyl adds no value to a home; it can take on a shoddy look when allowed to remain for too long.

HOW IT'S USED

As a residential product, vinyl is used primarily as flooring in heavy traffic areas, kitchens, and bathrooms. It is available in tile and sheet form, with the latter usually about twelve to fifteen feet wide.

Smooth, clean, and solid subflooring is very important. Any slight irregularity will form raised areas and create wear spots very quickly.

Tiles are much easier to install than sheet goods, and most homeowners are able to master the technique. Sheet goods are heavier and require precise cutting, usually with the aid of a preformed template of the area to be covered. The adhesive used for installation is not waterproof, and care should be taken that spills are removed promptly to preserve the integrity of the subfloor and adhesive.

FINISHING

Cleaning products like bleach can stain vinyl, as can rubber heels. Burns, either from cigarettes or hot cooking utensils, can cause permanent damage to vinyl as it is highly flammable. Standing water will damage the subfloor, and warping can occur.

Vinyl needs no sealing, waxing, or polishing. Once installed, it is virtually maintenance-free. Dusting and mopping are all the routine care needed to preserve the look and finish.

CARPET

Once the epitome of sumptuous interiors, carpet is a more accessible element of interior design than ever before. And it still hasn't lost its luxurious allure. Of all the classic elements

discussed, carpet, along with rugs and fabrics, is the most tactile and inviting. A carpet, by definition fitted wall-to-wall, can expand the sense of spaciousness in most rooms and works most effectively when covering expansive living spaces. Carpet remains very popular with every segment of the population. Young families with small children look to carpeting for softness and warmth for tiny hands and feet. For those of us who still love to roam around the house barefoot, carpeting is essential. Because carpet adds a small sound-dampening quality to most installations, it is invaluable in bedrooms. Changing the color or style of carpet from space to space also helps define different areas of most homes.

Carpet is made of many different fibers, pile constructions, backings, and densities, which affords a wide range of quality and price from which consumers can choose. In general, more expensive carpet, whether wool or man-made, is more durable and luxurious than cheap carpet, which wears badly and needs replacing far sooner than superior carpet.

Just the Facts

Carpet is soft underfoot, warm, and comfortable to live with. It can insulate against many loud sounds and impacts in the household.

Carpet comes in many grades for specific installations and areas of higher wear. Wool and wool-blend carpets are the most luxurious and durable.

Depending on composition and any applied treatments to the surface, carpet varies greatly in susceptibility to stains and spills. Mishaps should be attended to as soon as possible to ensure superior performance for the life of the carpet. Carpet can't withstand extended exposure to water. It is not recommended in kitchens, bathrooms, or other water areas.

Carpet comes in various widths, ranging from twenty-seven inches wide to over thirteen feet wide.

Carpet can harbor pet hair, mites, fleas, and other minute pests. Care should be taken to deep clean carpets if members of the family have allergies.

CONSTRUCTION

Woven carpets were the first machine-made carpets produced for mass consumption. The pile is woven into the backing in a similar way as handmade rugs. These carpets are long lasting and include types such as Axminster and Wilton, which have a pile on the surface and, quite often, colorful patterns. Flat weaves are also available with little or no pile.

Tufted carpets require the pile be inserted into the backing, which is then coated with adhesive to keep the tufts in place. A secondary backing may be added for extra strength. Tufts on the face of the carpet can be cut, left in loops, or a combination of the two to create interesting and enduring patterns and textures. Tufted carpet is generally of one color or a subtle blended shade.

Nonwoven carpets have fibers that are glued, flocked, or needle-punched to the backing. These carpets are available in roll and tile, have no pile, and are inexpensive. They become cheap looking in a very short time.

Durability is defined by how densely the fibers of a carpet are packed together. The tightness of the weave, not the depth, ensures long life for a carpet. If the carpet bounces back after pressed with your fingers, it's a good indication of tightness of weave. Pile weight is also a good indicator of durability. Light, domestic use for bedrooms and other lightly used rooms requires a pile weight of around one and three quarter pounds per square yard.

Light to medium use for living rooms requires a pile weight of around two pounds per square yard. Medium to heavy use for family rooms, stairways, and entries requires a pile weight of around two and a half pounds per square yard.

FIBERS

Wool is the most luxurious, softest, bulkiest, most expensive, and best performing of the fibers used for carpeting. It is available in many colors, and wool from New Zealand is especially good for carpet. Most wool is treated for moth protection before leaving the factory. Wool blends afford an even more durable product. Blended in a ratio of four parts wool to one part nylon, the result combines the appearance and comfort of wool with the superior durability of nylon.

Nylon is the most popular and widely used fiber for carpet in today's market. It is extremely durable, stainresistant, and available in a wide range of colors and styles. Good quality nylon is soft to the touch. As with any carpet, the denser the pile, the better the carpet will perform.

Polyester is often used in shag-style carpets for its soft, thick, cut-pile texture. It, too, is available in a wide range of colors.

Polypropylene (olefin) is a common fiber of inexpensive Berber style carpets and tends to flatten very easily. It is durable, stain resistant, and colorfast.

Acrylic is similar to wool in appearance and texture but is far more inexpensive. Acrylic is often used for velvet-pile carpets.

Viscose is used in the very cheapest of carpets and is easily soiled.

TYPES OF PILE

Cut piles are smooth with a matte finish and texture, which show footsteps more easily than other piles. Velvet-cut pile is a smoother, softer version of a simple cut pile and is hardwearing. It, too, shows footsteps.

Loop-pile carpets have uncut loops. The length of the loops determines whether the carpet will appear lighter or bulkier. Brussels weave is a tighter, more expensive version of the loop-pile carpet, and cord is a low-pile version that is very durable.

Berber is a style of carpet that employs the loop-pile technique with undyed, variegated, and flecked wool, which creates a bushy feel underfoot.

A mixture of cut and loop pile creates a pattern depending on how the height of the loop is juxtaposed against the flatness of the pile. Another very durable carpet.

For stairways, a fries-cut pile, in which the strands are tightly twisted to create a smoother texture, is a good choice, as it does not show footsteps and is hard wearing.

Shag piles, which have come and gone in popularity for years, are generally long strands, sometimes as much as two or even three inches, applied to a backing. Shag pile is difficult to keep clean, can cause trips and spills, is not suitable for heavy wear, and shouldn't be used on stairs.

INSTALLATION

Due to the weight and length of most rolls of carpet, a professional installer is always the best bet for an acceptable installation. The carpet must be stretched to lay flat and hug the edges of the space. Carpet should always be laid over a smooth, level, and dry subfloor. The base of some doors may have to be planed to allow for smooth opening and closing. Felt paper should be applied to subflooring before laying any type of carpet with a foam backing. This will ensure that the foam doesn't stick to the subfloor.

All fabric-backed carpets require some form of underlay or pad. With woven carpets, the best choice is a jute or jute-and-hair-combination pad. For tufted carpets, a noncrumbling foam pad of the newer generation padding works best.

MAINTENANCE

A stain-resistant topical application is usually applied at the factory, but a second application after installation is always a good idea. This is supplied by local carpet specialists or carpet retailers.

Carpet will shed fluff for the first few weeks of use and should not be overcleaned or over-vacuumed. Once the carpet has settled down, cleaning with a vacuum twice or even three times a week is recommended.

Always attend to spills and spots as soon as possible. Do not overwet the area, and never scrub too heavily. Treat water-based stains with mild detergent and water and oil-based spills with dry-cleaning fluids.

RUGS

With a plethora of styles, fibers, sizes, costs, and colors, area rugs are a staple of the interior design profession. Rugs help define an otherwise bland or unremarkable area and add warmth, underfoot comfort, and color to most interiors. Rugs are often used to define a seating area, in dining rooms, at entries, and along hallways. They also offer, like carpet, the added perk of sound dampening. Unlike carpet, rugs can be rotated to minimize wear, rolled up for storage, or moved to another area of the home.

It is generally not advised to place rugs over carpet. On hardwood or stone floors, a nonslip pad under the rug is important for safety and the longevity of the rug. The pad is essential to prevent wear at uneven areas of the flooring. Rugs should be swept or vacuumed regularly to prevent wear from dirt and grit. The fringe, if any, should also be gently brushed to retain a crisp, clean appearance. Although some cotton rugs can be washed, professional cleaning is recommended for most area rugs.

Rugs are available in a wide range of fibers, including nylon, silk, bamboo, cotton, and wool.

Just the Facts

There are a variety of wool rugs, some of which have been fabricated for centuries. Probably the most well-known are Persian rugs, which improve with age and last for centuries. These dense pile rugs are handwoven and generally made of wool or silk. The most well-known designs include garden of paradise, prayer arches, and tree of life, and there is a wide range of motifs and images associated

with the tribe from which the rug originates. There are also modern, machine-made versions of this style of rug, often made in wool/nylon blends or all man-made fiber. They don't have the panache of fine, handmade rugs and are far less expensive.

Chinese rugs are similar to Persian and made of wool or silk but are generally thicker and are quite often carved for a more stylistic interpretation.

Tibetan rugs are handknotted in wool and have a more rustic quality to their finish.

Turkish rugs are wool and come from the Middle and Near East. These, too, can be machine-made.

Turkoman and Bokhara rugs come from across Central Asia, are made of wool, and generally have a muted, almost dark, color palette.

Caucasian rugs are bright, less sophisticated than other Persian style rugs, and are often flat weave as opposed to knotted.

Kelims are flat-woven, coarse wool rugs made by the nomadic people of Afghanistan, Turkey, and Northern Africa. The patterns are almost always geometric in design, with colors ranging from black, deep red, blue, and cream. Good quality Kelim rugs can be very expensive.

Dhurries are cotton rugs woven in India into flat-weave, simple geometric patterns. These rugs are cheap, lend themselves to machine washing, and are generally reversible.

Serape rugs are similar to dhurries but flat woven of wool. The colors are bright and geometric.

Flokati is a Greek shag-pile rug in natural white or off-white wool.

Craft rugs are those made by the needlepoint method, hooked rugs, and braided rugs. The materials used are wool, cotton, and sometimes silk.

Contemporary rugs come in a huge range of styles, colors, and sizes. The materials used are almost anything available to today's interior designer. Wool, nylon, and cotton are the most widely used, with wool offering the very same qualities of luxury, durability, and quality one expects from carpet. There are many designers who have created name-brand lines for their rugs and these can be quite expensive but delightful to behold.

TEXTILES AND PAPERS

If it's true that carpets and rugs are the glamour-pusses of the design world, then fabrics and, to a lesser extent, papers are the true workhorses. Always colorful, fabrics benefited from improved printing techniques developed in the early 20th century. Exuberant prints and patterns emerged as designers and artists transferred natural elements to fabric and paper for use in homes. In England, the designers at Liberty re-envisioned arts and crafts elements as wall coverings and fabrics for mass consumption in the burgeoning middle-class homes spreading out from the central city to the suburbs.

Fabrics help manage noise in homes and are great insulators as fully lined drapery for windows. The selection today is enormous, and fabrics with matching wall coverings are everywhere. How a designer uses them and in what variety is the challenge. Most perform well when applied properly, and little care is required once installed.

On upholstery, fabric is essential for comfort and a warm sense of well-being. Whether it's wool, cotton, linen, nylon, or a mix, the right fabric will help define the style of the interior. Both drapery and upholstery, the largest uses of fabrics in the home, should be manufactured by talented amateurs or accomplished professionals. The care required to properly prepare a wood frame for upholstery and the meticulous detail involved with fine drapery and headers are not for the do-it-yourselfer.

Wall covering can also bring pattern and texture to a room. Today's extruded and expanded vinyl papers have a wealth of texture stamped into the pattern. These papers allow the designer to give a real punch to a room that might not be appropriate for heavy, textured wall finishes. Wallpaper also allows the designer the choice of pattern, style, and image with which to enhance any room.

Professional interior designers coordinate fabrics and papers, along with the other classic elements used in today's interiors, to create warm and inviting settings for families and friends.

Just the Facts

Fabrics and papers supply an immense range of patterns, textures, and colors for use in modern interior design. Many fabrics and papers offer the added option of varying texture, which is a prime element in the selection process. Many designs are available in both

fabric and paper form. Fabrics and papers can also be treated to help make them fire retardant and moisture resistant, and can help mitigate wear.

Choosing the appropriate weight for a specific job is very important, and often the use of a professional interior designer is advised. As with so many printed fabrics and papers, it is a good idea to get a cutting from stock before completing the order to ensure it matches the sample from which you are selecting the goods.

What to Look for in Fabrics

Choice of fabric will depend on the type of application and whether or not you want a pattern or a solid. Do you require a fabric that is sheerer for lightweight curtains, or is a print more desirable? Does the fabric need to be

machine washable, or must it be dry cleaned, and will that make a difference in your choice? View the fabric in natural light, and have a large enough sample to verify pattern repeat or any type of change in texture or color throughout the fabric. Always make sure you have adequate fabric to complete any job you might envision. Dye lots often change from piece to piece on fabrics.

TYPES OF FABRICS

Cotton is a versatile fiber and can be woven in a number of ways to create many types of fabrics for a multitude of uses. It is easily dyed and can be blended with other fibers, like nylon or linen, to create durable and highly usable fabrics.

Acetate is man-made fiber and is a wonderful substitute for silk when used on windows and other areas where fading might be a problem. It won't fade but may become brittle after a number of years.

Brocade is a luxurious fabric with a raised jacquard pattern and a sumptuous appearance, usually made of wool, cotton, silk, or a blend.

Canvas is a coarse cotton fabric or cotton-linen blend suitable for Roman shades, bedspreads, and areas in which heavier use demands a stronger fabric.

Chintz is a cotton fabric that is sometimes glazed to give a smooth and shiny appearance to the face. Chintz is a great choice for drapery and curtains and usually has a lively and colorful print.

Damask is a fabric in which the weave imparts a pattern woven into the piece. Damask is available in silk, cotton, linen, wool, and a variety of man-made fibers.

Dupion was originally Indian silk but is now more often made of acetate or viscose.

Gingham is cotton fabric with a check pattern and is used most often for homey and rustic interiors.

Lace has a delicate, open style and was once only available handmade, which made it a costly material indeed. Today, modern machine-made lace is widely used for window treatments, bedding, and tablecloths.

Linen is the natural fiber made from the flax plant. Linen is strong but creases easily. Blending with cotton makes it less prone to creasing, and when used on upholstery, it often has no crease problem at all.

Moire, also know as watered silk, has a wavy, slightly raised pattern and comes in a wealth of colors.

Muslin is a cheap, lightweight, sheer cotton fabric, used often for billowy curtains and bedding. It is also used as lining for some drapery treatments.

Polyester is man-made and hangs well when made into drapery.

Silk is made from the spun silk of moths. Silk has a strong tensile strength, colors beautifully, can be woven into many different patterns, and is soft to the touch. Fine silk fabrics with beautiful printing or

weaving techniques can be expensive. Silk also tends to dry-rot when exposed to direct sunlight. It is not suggested for window treatments unless heavily lined.

Silk taffeta is a crisp form of silk and is often used to create imaginative window treatments that have a "ball gown" sensibility to them.

Velvet, whether cotton, silk, or linen, is a sumptuous fabric with a deep, inviting pile and a durability to rival many of the man-made fabrics available today.

Wool is often woven into very fine weights that easily lend themselves to drapery treatments. It can also be woven into heavier tweeds and, when mixed with nylon or cotton, is suitable for upholstery.

HOW THEY'RE USED

Fabrics are extraordinarily versatile and, in the right hands, can be used to create interiors that invite, excite, and invigorate. There is almost nothing fabrics can't do in an interior. Depending on which fiber is chosen, the fabric selected can be manufactured into drapery, upholstery, cushions, pillows, bedspreads, comforters, and table linens. Fabric is often used on walls to create an elegant envelope in a dining room or to control sound and noise in an office environment. In fact, the possibilities are almost limitless.

Wallpaper: Choosing and Hanging

Like printed fabrics, wallpaper comes in a massive variety of colors and styles. Choosing the right paper is often best left to a professional interior designer. He or she will know just what weight, style, and color is right for a particular setting. Although many people have tried to install wallpaper them-

selves, it is still most often better to choose a professional installer for the job.

The wallpaper must be applied over a clean, smooth wall that has been prepared with an oil-based sealer or preparation suggested by the manufacturer. Wallpaper should never be applied over existing wallpaper or a painted wall that isn't properly prepared. Lining paper is often a good choice to ensure a smooth, even surface for the chosen wallpaper. Many more expensive screen-printed papers come untrimmed and must have the edges cut straight and smoothed before installation.

Machine-printed papers are by far the most available types on the market today. These papers use a photogravure or rotor-press printing technique, are low in quality, and are very cheap.

Screen-printed papers are the choice of most professional interior designers and offer crisp, unique designs in multiple colors. The cost of the paper will depend on the number of colors in the paper, as each color must be run and dried before the next color is applied. This silk-screen technique uses patterns cut into a silk screen, over which a layer of gel has been applied to block ink. Each color chosen to create the

pattern requires an additional screen to be cut. The technique is manufactured either with machines or by hand. These papers are generally untrimmed.

Hand-printed papers, also referred to as block-printed papers, use individual blocks, to which ink is applied. The blocks are then pressed onto the paper. This technique is time-consuming and costly.

Natural-fiber papers, such as grass cloth, burlap, and jute, are paper backed, then applied to the surface just like any other paper.

Double-width papers are also available, usually for commercial applications.

There are no standards in size and shape of a roll of paper, but generally, wallpapers come in an American roll, which is usually twenty-seven inches wide and five yards long. These are most often sold two or three rolls to the piece and are referred to as double or triple rolls. European rolls are twenty-one inches wide and eleven yards long. These are also usually packed and sold in double-roll bolts. When measuring for wallpaper, know what type of roll you will be using for the installation.

PART TWO

UPDATED AND DURABLE: CONTEMPORARY

No single event in the history of mankind had a more profound effect on the socioeconomic and cultural conditions of the time than what is called the industrial revolution. Dating from about 1770 to the late 1800s, this momentous event changed the way goods were manufactured and distributed across the globe. The transition from manual labor to machine-based manufacturing produced a dramatic increase in production capacity. It also created a large and wealthy middle class, which in turn created the need for interior design services. Interior design as we know it today is a direct result of the industrial revolution.

By the late 1800s, designers and furniture makers began to look at the manufactured materials used in industrial and commercial installations as worthy of use in more residential settings. This was the creation of modernism, and it reflected a new and vigorous approach to residential interior design. This creative crossover was led by the Bauhaus school of design and men like Le Corbusier, Mies van der Rohe, and Charles and Ray Eames. By the turn of the 20th century, Scottish designers like Charles Rennie Mackintosh and Eileen Gray embraced the new aesthetic.

The fundamental change in this new minimalism was the use of manufactured materials developed for their utility, not necessarily their beauty. The Exposition Internationale des Arts Decoratifs et Industrials Modernes in Paris in 1925 combined beautifully the functional, elegant, glamorous, and modern in a way never before seen. Art Deco's linear symmetry was a radical departure from the flowing and soft lines

of Art Nouveau and embraced the use of modern materials like chrome, stainless steel, stone, and precious metals.

Today's modern aesthetic, to some extent, comes from the recent trend to reuse, renovate, and restore. Think carriage houses as apartments, lofts as homes, and factories as multi-use properties. With exposed walls of brick and vast expanses of concrete flooring, there was a need for more robust and muscular forms within the interiors. Designers turned to the very same materials used in interior spaces that were appropriate to the space and warm and livable for the inhabitants.

Although some argued these spaces could be warm and inviting, modern designers still shied away from soft and homey materials, with the attendant clutter. The new designs were sleek and angular. With cavernous spaces and hard surfaces, the employment of rugs and fabric became important sound control, but with a twist. Shipping blankets became upholstery material, wooden pallets became bed frames, and mesh grids became refined and elegant design materials.

These materials also changed with time and continue to change. Concrete became lighter in weight and, in some instances, almost transparent. Glass was improved with double glazing, new colors, and the ability to provide privacy from the outside world. None of this would have happened without the demand of designers and their clients. Designers have embraced the new age with wit and a desire to employ the best of whatever is available, irrespective of its provenance. Rubber floors, photoceramics, decorative glass, and metal fabrics are just some of the many examples of the new and innovative materials available to today's professional interior designer.

CONCRETE

What was once used in residential architectural design for foundations and subfloors has come from behind the walls and under the house to become a pleasing and important part of modern interior design. Best remembered for its use in dreary utilitarian parking garages and unsightly apartment blocks, concrete has been transformed through the use of sophisti-cated color and finishing techniques to be the main attraction in many residences around the globe.

Avant-garde interior designers and architects began using exposed concrete as a final interior finish some decades ago, and most of them have never looked back. The bold, muscular look of concrete is what appealed to designers for use in pared-down minimalist interiors. The very energy it exudes gives new life and interest to otherwise empty and bland interiors.

In the right setting, with the right finish, concrete countertops and work surfaces take on an almost monumental beauty, completing the interior design.

With new techniques, concrete can be molded to form bathtubs, sinks, and other vessels within the home. Floors and walls take on a new depth and a sense of the elemental with improved incising and casting techniques, and the lighter weight of today's concrete makes it an easy-to-install alternative to stone.

Just the Facts

Concrete is cheap to produce, easily molded into various shapes, and very strong. Like stone, it absorbs and releases heat slowly and is often used in areas for passive solar heat loss and gain.

The many attributes of concrete are functions of the basic mix. Sand, water, gravel, and Portland cement are combined to achieve different densities, weights, performance characteristics, and appearances. Some environmentalists suggest using fly ash, a by-product of coal-powered factories, instead of Portland cement to reduce carbon dioxide emissions.

Concrete is fireproof and virtually indestructible when properly fabricated. Although cold and hard, it is naturally moisture and insect resistant.

If not sealed properly, it can stain easily, but otherwise requires little or no maintenance.

Concrete can be laid on-site and is also available precast into slabs, blocks, tiles, and thin wall panels.

Lighter concrete blocks have a better insulation quality than heavier blocks, and newer, translucent concrete allows light into otherwise dark interiors.

Concrete should be mixed by professionals, and protective clothing should always be worn when working around fresh concrete as it can burn the skin if splashed.

Concrete must cure fully before it can be used and should be treated if exposed to prevent it from continually shedding or breaking down into fine particles.

Cast On-Site

The vast majority of concrete used in residential construction is cast on the site where the final product will be used. For new construction, the need for a spacious area in which to fabricate the concrete, move it to the site of the pour, and let it cure for up to four weeks is not a problem. When the material is to be used in an existing interior, the challenge of where and how to mix, move, and pour the material is exacerbated by close-in walls and existing finishes that need protection.

A professional or very experienced do-it-yourselfer is the best choice to fabric the mix of sand, water aggregate, and cement. Too little sand or too much water and the concrete will be too dense and possibly not strong enough. Too much cement will cause cracking as the material dries.

Different types and proportions of aggregate (sand and gravel) also affect the appearance. The more aggregate in the mix, the less dense the finished product. Standard concrete is gray; whiter concrete is made using white cement and white gravel.

QUALITIES

Concrete can be transformed into a structural material by pouring it over steel rods, wire, or mesh. It is used extensively for foundations and structural supports. Although concrete sets in hours, it takes up to a month to cure properly, and some areas might have to be out of bounds for a time. The temperatures in these areas must be stable and well over freezing at all times in the curing process. Concrete will not set if mixed on or near the freezing point.

Concrete can be colored by adding pigments to the base mix as it is manufactured. It also stains easily.

Mixing cement with water causes a chemical reaction and the wet concrete, if splashed onto the skin, can burn.

HOW IT'S USED

Concrete is used to create foundations and smooth subfloors for heavier materials such as stone and ceramic and can be used as the finished flooring, as well. Poured with mixed-in color and a smooth finish surface, concrete creates warm and interesting flooring. Concrete is suitable for an underfloor-heating element.

Concrete can be poured into molds and allowed to set. The molds, usually wooden or possibly metal, support the concrete while it sets and is then removed. Various patterns, shapes, and textures can be worked into the mold to create an imprint on the finished item.

Concrete is used for countertops, floors, sinks, tubs, tables, and work surfaces.

FINISHING

A smooth surface is achieved by finishing with a sand and cement layer.

Elements of all kinds—stone, shell, and glass—can be inserted into the wet cement and, when honed, become a feature of the final installation. This is used very effectively on countertops and in sinks and tubs. Special floor paints in a wide range of color add to the design choices available for concrete finishing.

Concrete is porous and should be sealed with a self-leveling acrylic or epoxy resin for a glossy, strong, and chemical-resistant finish.

Concrete can be made nonslip with the application of industrial toppings applied by a professional.

Tiles, Panels, and Blocks

Concrete elements that are cast off site, or precast, are attractive and usually meant to be seen. In this manageable form, concrete is far easier to use; it cuts time on-site, and there is no need to wait for the concrete to cure. It is a far less messy and disruptive process. Still, working with precast cement does require some strength and a certain amount of skill for the installations.

Decorative concrete tiles are available in a wide range of color and shape. They can be used outdoors for patios, pathways, and edging or indoors as flooring. Textures may be honed smooth or ribbed, and the grouting can be part of the overall color or a contrast shade.

With computer control, fine etching, and carving techniques, there are many patterns and textures available for concrete tiles. Many of these tiles are made to order and as such are more expensive than simple concrete tiles, but they come with the added caché of the artisan's touch. Incised concrete can be installed on walls and backsplashes. When sealed properly, it can also be used for flooring, but it requires more maintenance and can be uneven underfoot.

QUALITIES

Concrete block is lighter in weight due to its honeycomb design. It is also higher in insulation properties and is well suited for exterior walls, partitions, and small structures. Concrete tiles can be textured to resemble stone, colored to match any interior design, and come in various thicknesses.

Large slabs for external use are thicker and weather resistant. Thinner tiles are used like ceramic and stone tiles, are thinner than exterior tiles, and are installed on a solid subfloor with mortar or grout between the joints. Panels of precast concrete come in a range of thicknesses and can be used for exterior and interior applications. Although thin tiles of concrete can be attached with adhesives, thicker panels must be secured in place by metal supports.

How It's Used

Concrete block is installed with mortar and placed in a pattern similar to brick. By placing the honeycomb interior facing out, a panel or wall takes on the semitransparent aspects of a screen; this is very effective for garden walls and exterior partitions.

With flooring, the subfloor must be strong enough to bear the weight of the concrete tiles or slabs and must be smooth, dry, and even. The addition of pattern or color will enhance the rather bland and basic look of unadorned concrete flooring.

Although any concrete tile or slab can be used to clad indoor walls, for the most effective expression of interior design, the most interesting are the handmade artisan-style tiles.

Finishing

Little or no finishing is required on concrete beyond sealing, if needed, and the application of paint or other topping for interest.

Concrete, untreated with a topical finish, can stain.

Translucent Concrete

Not transparent, but beautifully translucent, this concrete element has transformed the way we literally "see" concrete. Thousands of optical glass fibers form a matrix and run parallel to each other between the two main surfaces of each block. The proportion of the fibers is very small (4 percent) compared to the total volume of the blocks. Moreover, these fibers mingle in the concrete because of their insignificant size and become a structural component as a kind of modest aggregate. Therefore, the surface of the blocks remains homogeneous concrete. With the brand name Litracon™, invented by Aron Losonczi, this innovative product has stretched the way concrete can be used both structurally and aesthetically.

QUALITIES

Translucent concrete is available in various sizes in both block and panel. Patterns and designs can be specified for interior design requirements.

Performance, structurally, is similar to standard concrete block.

The fibers used transmit light for up to sixty feet, which means walls can be several feet thick with no appreciable loss of translucence.

HOW IT'S USED

Used to create external or internal walls or screens, translucent concrete brings light into otherwise windowless rooms. Light is intensified when used on east- or west-facing sides due to the lower angle of natural light in the morning and evening. Interior panels are effective when backlit and convey an almost shimmering effect.

Advanced Cast Concrete

These newer concrete manifestations are a mixing of natural silica sands and complex cement mixtures. Although strong and dense, the material has a lightweight core and is just as durable as stone but far less heavy.

This element is produced as panels, counters, stairs, and other features, which can be produced to individual specifications and can be installed with a minimum of disruption to existing interior installations. The concrete is available in a multitude of colors and finishes with a high-tech feel and a sleek, updated sensibility. Advanced cast concrete is polished and sealed at the factory and is ready for installation upon delivery to the site.

QUALITIES

Advanced cast concrete comes in lightweight panels of various sizes and thicknesses. The surface is cooler than laminate and warmer than stone. It is lighter and easier to install than on-site casting, and provides limitless design possibilities and finishes.

HOW IT'S USED

Advanced cast concrete can be used in kitchen and bath countertops; it can be ordered with precut openings for ranges, sinks, and faucets and can be incised with drainage grooves. The pieces are often supplied with install-ready backing and are easy to slip into place.

The surface is heat resistant, antimicrobial, and resists staining when properly sealed.

Thin cladding sheets are available for vertical installations on walls. Stairs and risers with curves and angles are available in a wide range of finishes and colors. Furniture pieces, shelves, hearths, backsplashes, doorframes, and other elements can all be made out of this material.

FINISHING

Most manufacturers prefinish and seal the material for heat and stain resistance.

Terrazzo

Terrazzo is the up-market cousin of cement floors. Although widely used in commercial applications throughout the world, it is particularly welcome in residential settings in warmer climates. Due to its inherent hardness, terrazzo has been used in retail stores, supermarkets, and offices since the mid-20th century. It has also been used residentially in the American Southwest and other southern states for many years.

The composition is basically the same as concrete: a combination of cement and aggregate. With terrazzo, however, the true design aesthetic is achieved with the use of colored glass, marble, and colored granite chips placed throughout the material during pouring. All the elements help create a luminous and inviting finish.

In many residential settings, terrazzo is mixed and poured on-site, after which brass or other metal strips are placed for expansion and contraction. Terrazzo is then ground smooth, filled with resins or paste to seal imperfections and create a perfectly smooth surface, and finally allowed to cure. It is then polished to a high sheen.

Precast tiles are far easier to install, but both applications require the help of a professional installer. These tiles are placed on a smooth subfloor and separated by brass or zinc dividers.

QUALITIES

Terrazzo is hard, cold, and noisy. Items that fall will break, as with stone flooring. But it is a blessing in warm and hot climates, as it retains its coolness.

Although there are many iterations of terrazzo, most have a lighter background with a mottled pattern derived from the aggregates used to form the material. Some handmade tiles are also available with specific mixes of aggregate for bespoke flooring looks.

As with other tiles, patterns and motifs can be created by using a mix of colors and finishes.

Terrazzo is almost as costly as stone, and when laid on-site, it is more expensive than tiles. But it is very durable and often worth the expense.

Terrazzo is nonslip unless highly polished or wet.

HOW IT'S USED

Terrazzo is used primarily for flooring in kitchens, entries, bathrooms, and hallways. It is also used throughout many homes in warmer and hotter geographic areas of both the United States and other parts of the world.

FINISHING

Terrazzo is sealed with a water-based topical application to prevent stains. Wax polishes should be avoided as they can make the terrazzo slippery. Wash with warm water and a nonsoapy cleanser. Soap leaves a slippery film.

METAL

Man first began to fashion metal into items for personal use as early as the Bronze Age, dating from around 3500 BC For more than 5,000 years, we have experimented with different types of amalgams and recipes to create strong and durable items from metal. As we began to create buildings and homes, metal was used in the form of nails, hinges, screws, knobs, and fixtures as well as for railings and fire screens. It is only recently, however, that we have begun to use more metal in structural and aesthetic ways. Modern interiors include the juxtaposition of metal against glass to create clean, almost ethereal spaces. As recently as a few decades ago, metal was still considered an industrial element and not particularly suited to residential interiors. Not any more. The benefits of unique finishes, airy open railings, and great strength relative to size all combine to give metal an undeniable élan in our homes. Metal and metal finishes have become very chic. Stainless steel kitchens exude a functional cachet with an almost hygienic aesthetic. Metal as an element of interior design is crisp, clean, and easy to use.

Just the Facts

Metal has great strength. All metals are durable and pest resistant. As a structural material, metal can be expensive, but due to its strength, less material is required, thereby reducing overall costs.

Base metals react to the elements and many can rust over time. Iron, aluminum, and lead are base metals and are manufactured into many elements we use in our home every day.

Noble metals, such as gold, silver, platinum, and copper, don't rust, but can tarnish over time, often with beautiful results. The use of protective applications helps those metals that rust and corrode retain their original finish.

All types of metal conduct electricity and gain and lose heat very quickly and easily.

Metal amplifies sounds and contributes to an excessive noise level if not properly balanced with softer, more sound-absorbent materials.

Metal is relatively easy to recycle. In many instances, more than 90 percent of most metal can be recycled for new uses.

Iron

The Iron Age followed the Bronze Age as iron became the superior metal for weapons and tool manufacturing. Iron ore, which is found throughout the world, is relatively easy to mine, smelt, and fabricate into usable items for use by man.

Pig iron, which is smelted in a furnace at over 2,300 degrees Fahrenheit to extract the ore, is the most basic form of iron. Steel is composed of almost 99 percent pig iron.

Cast iron is formed by pouring the molten metal into molds and allowing it to cool. Cast iron is brittle but is more resistant to corrosion than wrought iron. Wrought iron is strong and can be pulled, twisted, and hammered into many different shapes. Although most iron today is cast, wrought iron was used extensively before the age of industrialization. To make wrought iron, iron oxide is added to pig iron to purify it

and make it less liquid. Blacksmiths fabricated wrought iron into items as mundane as horseshoes and as elaborate as majestic gates and fences for large country homes. Today, the use of wrought iron is chiefly limited to decorative applications in the home.

Corrugated iron, invented in Britain in the 1820s, is sheet iron that is crimped, or corrugated, to add strength. It has become widely used in functional outbuildings on farms and temporary structures throughout the world.

Many sheet metals, such as steel, which are formed into corrugated forms are referred to as corrugated iron.

QUALITIES

Iron has a high melting point and is exceptionally hard. It is heavy, abundant, and cheap to manufacture. It is easy to recycle but must be protected to prevent corrosion.

HOW IT'S USED

Iron is particularly useful for period restorations in the form of handles, hinges, knobs, fire surrounds, pokers, and fire irons.

Iron was used extensively in the late 19th century as exposed structural beams and columns and is found today in reclaimed warehouses and buildings from that period.

Iron is still used today as railings and for spiral staircases in its cast form.

FINISHING

When used outdoors, iron, like all base metals, is highly prone to corrosion unless

protected with paint or lacquer finishes. Many corrugated metals are protected with a galvanized coating or zinc plating to increase their resistance to rust and corrosion. Painting gives these metals full protection from the elements.

Steel

Steel, an iron alloy with less than 2 percent carbon, is one of the most common materials in the world, with more than 1.3 billion tons produced annually. It is a major component in buildings, infrastructure, tools, ships, automobiles, machines, appliances, and weapons.

With the invention of the Bessemer process in the mid-19th century, steel became an inex-

pensive, mass-produced material. Steel frameworks have allowed buildings to become taller and lighter. Masonry walls have been replaced with glass by using steel as the support for upper stories. Carbon steel is the most common type of steel and is used primarily in the building industry. There are many other forms of steel, however, which are formed into alloys that contain, among other materials, manganese, vanadium, or chromium.

Stainless steel is the glamour-puss of the group, and its most iconic use was to clad the Chrysler Building in New York City in 1930. The alloy contains chromium and nickel and is

resistant to rust and easy to maintain. Stainless steel is also the most expensive type of steel, but it is valued for its luster and numerous finish possibilities.

With the addition of other metals, steel can be hardened to impact (manganese), resistant to high temperatures (tungsten), and weather-proofed by a layer of zinc, aluminum, or both.

QUALITIES

Steel is much stronger than iron, but like iron, it is susceptible to corrosion unless mixed as an alloy. It is pliable and easy to manufacture into various shapes and forms. With different alloys and finishes, steel is used in almost every facet of daily life. Texturing, ridging, and corrugating increase the structural strength of steel. It has been recycled for years.

HOW IT'S USED

Steel is used primarily as structural material, from beams to studs to load-bearing elements. It can be used to create custom-made steel stairways and spiral staircases, as well as flooring and cladding for buildings, appliances, and cabinets. Steel is also used in sinks, lavatories, faucets, handles, and a wealth of other interior features.

FINISHES

Steel is available in a number of coatings to resist rust and corrosion. Generally, when used indoors, steel will not rust.

Stainless steel shows water spots and greasy streaks. A manufacturer-approved cleaning product will restore the material to a factory finish.

Aluminum

Well known for its use in the aviation industry, aluminum is second only to iron in its many uses worldwide. Within the home, it is used as structural elements, from studs for walls to doors and siding.

QUALITIES

Aluminum has a dull, silvery appearance and can be polished to a high sheen. It is lightweight and resistant to corrosion. Aluminum is soft and malleable, a good conductor of heat and electricity, and is nonmagnetic.

Anodized aluminum has a porous surface and can be dyed into a variety of colors.

Heat-tempered aluminum is as strong and resilient as steel.

HOW IT'S USED

Aluminum is used in industrial applications, such as a treaded flooring. It is either screwed or glued in place over a solid, smooth subfloor. It can be found in windows and doorframes, blinds and dividers, lightweight furniture, and small-scale applications.

FINISH

Aluminum is highly resistant to corrosion and requires no treatment except basic maintenance.

111

GLASS

Developments in the manufacturing process in the early 20th century transformed glass from a handmade, expensive product to a readily accessible, affordable commodity. In the mid-20th century, the use of glass in residential settings became one of the most important aspects of contemporary architecture and interior design. The desire was to literally bring the outdoors in and create spaces that flowed easily from indoors out. Glazing was its primary use until recently. Now sinks (known as vessels in the trade), flooring, panels, room dividers, and other objects have brought glass into many facets of our daily lives. Float glass is the most prevalent type and is produced by pouring molten glass into a vat of molten tin, where it levels off, cools, and hardens. The glass is then moved to an annealing oven for final hardening. The result is a uniformly level and clear piece of glass.

Just the Facts

Although many glasses look the same, there is a vast range of types of glass available in today's marketplace. It is important to work with a professional to ascertain the best choice for the type of glass to be used in any project.

Glass is available in a wide range of colors, sizes, and performance characteristics. Size is determined more by shipping and packing restraints than difficulty in fabrication.

Most glass requires a good deal of maintenance to keep its clear, clean appearance. Self-cleaning glass reduces the maintenance to a large degree.

Large expanses of glass heat a room during the day and in warmer weather; in the evening and in cold weather, heat dissipates.

Glass is easy to recycle without any loss to its integrity.

Strengthened Glass

The more recent innovations in glassmaking have focused on giving it more strength and less fragility. Safety has also been of concern, and glass now has properties that make it less likely to shatter into sharp shards that can cut and puncture.

One of the cheapest forms of strengthened glass is wired glass. Created by pressing two panes of glass on either side of a wire mesh, this type of glass holds pieces in place when shattered and offers an increased amount of security.

Tempered glass is formed by applying high heat, approximately 1,200 degrees Fahrenheit, then chilling rapidly. As the outer surface cools, the inner layer is still warm and as it cools, the outer layers are compressed. It is far stronger than standard glass and when impacted shatters into small, harmless pieces. It cannot be cut or worked when finished so must be cast to size.

Laminated glass combines a layer of plastic inserted between two layers of glass. On impact, this glass holds its pieces in place. It was developed for car windshields and side windows and is effective in preventing injuries from glass shards in accidents.

Honeycombed glass incorporates honeycombed aluminum, is very light, rigid, and strong enough to be used structurally and as flooring.

How It's Used

Glass can be a combination of the different types of strengthened and is used for almost any type of application. Laminated glass is used throughout the home for windows, sliding doors, and French doors for safety and durability. One risk associated with glass is its transparent quality, which can lead to an accidental walk-through. One remedy is using shaded, frosted, or incised glass.

Glass used for walkways, stairs, and flooring is generally made up of one top layer of glass laminated to a second thicker layer. An option is honeycombed glass. In these applications, sandblasting or cutting small bars in the glass reduces the chance of slips and falls.

Beams made of glass offer support for glazed roofs and offer a wonderful transparent look.

Glass is particularly beguiling when used in bathrooms; shower enclosures, sinks, and tubs made of glass offer a refreshing alternative to porcelain.

Countertops, vanity tops, and the like can be polished, sandblasted, or ribbed to create varied effects, with the edges roughly chipped or smoothly polished. The choice is up to the designer.

Decorative Glass

The whole point of glass, of course, is its transparency, but there are times when it can be unsafe or become a privacy issue. In these instances, colored or shaded glass is a good choice and contributes to the design scheme in the way of pattern, texture, or color.

Colored glass is an excellent choice for areas in which privacy is not an issue. In these instances, color can be added via paint, through the use of metal oxides when fabricating, or by using a layer of colored plastic for the inter-layer of laminated glass. Light levels are lowered and the glass tends to absorb heat. Interiors are cooler. Large panels or simple slivers of decorative glass will add color and interest to otherwise dreary areas by creating sparkles of color and shadow. These types of glass give privacy without blocking too much light. They are particularly effective for bath-room windows, shower enclosures, and front and rear doors.

Decorative glass is more visible and therefore safer than clear glass because it is easier to notice. Decorative glass can be used for dividers, cabinet doors in kitchens, baths, vanity tops, back-splashes, and countertops.

Opaque glass is translucent rather than transparent and comes in various levels of opacity. The light coming through is not blocked but simply diffused. The surface is either acid etched or sandblasted, and many designs are one-of-a-kind with beautifully realized patterns and styles for more decorative effects.

Patterned or screen-printed glass adds another dimension to the designer's palette. Transparent or opaque inks designed specifically for use with glass are available.

Textured glass uses relief patterns or surface texture and reduces transparency and distorts views. The design for this glass is either rolled on as the glass cools or is actually created when the glass is cast. New, high-performance textured glass comes in an array of beautiful patterns and can be custom designed to fit any decor. This newer glass is relatively nonslip and is a wonderful alternate for flooring on walkways and stairs.

Colored laminated safety glass is particularly effective when used in conjunction with structural elements such as balcony railings, windows, doors, and countertops. It provides a high degree of safety, as the pieces adhere to the vinyl sheeting if accidents occur. Colored laminated safety glass is available in more than a thousand colors and shades and is a breathtaking addition to most interiors.

Another alternative to large, heavy, and unwieldy sheets of glass is the use of a profiled glass system. Using an aluminum frame lined with plastic, small (panels) panes, of glass are inserted and joined by flanges manufactured into the panes to achieve an interesting and translucent wall.

Adding lighting to the support tracks adds another dimension to the panes. The use of colored gels creates an even wash of light that can be dimmed, highlighted, or turned off as needed. The screen becomes self-supporting, with the channels arranged either horizontally or vertically. Like all other glass, the panes are available in any length and thickness, with a wide range of colors available.

Glass blocks combine transparency with strength and can be used in many different contexts, outdoors or in. As a contemporary design element, glass block has become something of a cliché, but new and improved manufacturing and installation techniques have given the element new life in the interior design world.

Installation is best performed by a professional. The blocks are strong, durable, secure, and come in a wide choice of color and finish. The blocks, generally square, can be formed into curves as well as straight walls, but care should be taken to provide proper support for the weight of the blocks en masse. Blocks used underfoot, either outdoors or in, can provide illumination to lower areas that otherwise might not have access to natural light.

Mirror

Mirror has been used for centuries to provide the practical help needed in personal hygiene. Today, however, using large expanses of mirror helps create depth of view and increased light within our personal spaces. The depth, or negative space, provided creates the illusion of

expanded space within the context of the interior.

QUALITIES

Like glass, mirror is available in a wide range of sizes, shapes, and colors. The style of framed mirrors is usually expressed by the framing. The larger the mirror, the heavier it is. Mirror shatters easily, and modern acrylic mirror is available in large sheets. The acrylic mirror is lighter in weight, easily cut on-site, and shatterproof.

Heated mirrors, for use in bathrooms where steam is present, prevent fogging and keep the image clear for use.

Mirrored furniture and cabinetry were particularly popular in the early 20th century and are still available today.

HOW IT'S USED

Mirror is decorative and used throughout residential interiors. Plain, frameless mirror in large sheets can be cut for use as cladding on entire walls, backsplashes, and alcoves needing the depth the mirror provides. Professional installation is recommended for large sheets of glass.

Mirror tile is available but is not recommended for use on large areas.

FINISHING

Mirror needs no subsequent finishing once it is installed.

Like glass, mirror needs routine maintenance with a dry cloth and window cleaner.

SYNTHETIC MATERIALS

Although many synthetics are completely man-made, there are many combinations, or composites, available today that combine the best of nature with the best of man. It was only after World War II that plastics and composites became part of our everyday world. Plastic is so ubiquitous in our homes, from light switches to tables to weatherproof membranes, that we sometimes forget there was a time when none of this existed. Plastic is heavily oil dependent but are also easily recycled. Many plastics and composites were originally designed for other uses, but we have transformed them for use in our homes.

Plastics are colorful, lightweight, and easily installed.

Acrylic

Acrylic was part of the first wave of thermo-plastics developed just after World War II. It becomes soft when heated and hardens to retain its shape when cool. It can be molded into innumerable shapes and used as sheets for windows and openings. It can be mixed with pigments, natural materials, and fillers to mimic the look of granite and other stones.

QUALITIES

Acrylic is lightweight and durable. Its strength varies according to its thickness. Acrylic doesn't fade in sunlight and can be formed into transparent, opaque, or translucent sheets. It can also be spun into fibers and is used extensively today for outdoor fabrics, where its fade-resistant qualities are very desirable.

How They're Used

Large sheets of acrylic are lighter than glass and far easier to install. They are widely used in bathroom sinks, tubs, and shower trays.

As stated, acrylic fabrics are fade resistant, soft, colorful, and easily cleaned. Even bleach will not harm the fabric.

Finishing

Once acrylic is installed or applied, cleaning with a soft cloth and nonabrasive cleaner is recommended.

Composites and Quartz Stones

Composite stones and solid composite materials are available under a number of brand names. Corian® is used for countertops and other areas in which hygiene and high performance are required. Through-colored and easy to install, it is almost seamless due to the large sheet sizes and custom-design capabilities available. Other brand names of solid composite material are also available through home stores and designers.

Zodiaq® uses natural stone, almost 92 percent, and resins to form a seamless hard surface for countertops and other work surfaces. Slightly cheaper than natural stone and available is many colors, Zodiaq® and other quartz composites perform as well, if not better, than their natural counterparts.

How They're Used

Composite stones are nontoxic, hypoallergenic, and antibacterial. They are nonporous

and stain and moisture resistant. Professional installation is suggested.

FINISHING

Once installed, no additional finish
is needed on composite stones. Clean
with a soft, damp cloth.

Composite stones are heat resistant,
but the use of trivets or cutting boards is
recommended. Never directly cut or
chop on either surface.

Decorative Laminate

Decorative laminate is composed of
layers of paper, up to 60 percent,
impregnated with thermosetting resins

and bonded under high pressure and heat. The top layer of paper contains the pattern or image used to finish the product. Available in almost any color and style, laminate is stronger and more fire resistant than thermoplastics.

Formica® has become the generic term for this type of laminate and is the leading product in the category. Many items manufactured in the 1940s are valued for their retro quality and style.

QUALITIES

The finished product can mimic wood, stone, and metal, with a huge variety of colors and finishes available.

Laminate is graded depending on its use, with higher grades used for countertops and work areas. The use of the wrong grade can result in poor performance, and the advice of a professional is recommended.

Laminate is hygienic and low maintenance, but poor-quality laminate is not wearresistant; it can delaminate over time and should be avoided.

How It's Used

Laminate is used for kitchen countertops, backsplashes, vanities, tabletops, shelving, wall cladding, and work stations.

Store laminate in the area where it will be installed to allow for acclimatization.

Finishing

Once installed, laminate requires no further finishing. Wipe clean with water and a soft cloth. Do not use abrasive cleaners or furniture polish. Textured surfaces can be cleaned with a nylon brush and gentle cleaner.

Sheet Resin

Cast resin can provide luminous colors and fascinating images depending on how it is colored and what is inserted between the layers. The panels or sheets are lightweight and easily handled and installed.

Qualities

Design and style are defined by what is placed in the interior layers of the resin. The designer can choose gossamer textiles, thin three-dimensional objects like grass, leaves, or petals, or a combination of each. The panels can be lit either from the back or front.

They can be translucent, clear, or frosted and are easily worked with woodworking tools.

The material is available in a wide range of sizes and thicknesses.

HOW IT'S USED

Sheet resin is used in vertical elements like screens, partitions, dividers, and feature wall cladding. It can also be used for shelving, light-use counters, and tabletops.

FINISHING

No further finish is required on resin once installed. Use a soft cloth and nonabrasive cleaner.

Rubber

Don't be surprised to find rubber among man-made items. The element we refer to as rubber is made up of a synthetic called SBR rubber, which is a petrochemical derivative. Used in the 1980s as a strong, no-nonsense flooring for airports, hospitals, and other heavy traffic areas, rubber has become popular in contemporary residential settings and is available in as many as seventy colors and patterns.

Tiles of approximately twenty-four square inches and about an eighth of an inch thick are the usual choice for most residential installations. Like ceramic tiles and other flooring, a smooth, strong subfloor is required for proper installation. A professional installer is best for this type of job.

Rubber is soft, warm, tactile, and feels very soft underfoot, even though it is incredibly strong. It is antibacterial, antistatic, and nonslip. It resists cigarette burns and can be used over underfloor heating.

Cleaning with a mixture of water and a small amount of vinegar keeps the rubber looking like new.

Rubber can be used in kitchens, bathrooms, entryways, and utility rooms. When designed for outdoor use, its nonslip attributes make it a good choice for poolside and other wet areas.

TILES

Tile, as an element, can take on many forms and be made from many different products. Ceramic tiles are the most widely used, but leather, glass, and even pebbles are choices designers have to work with. Tile is humanly scaled, so it is a natural choice for nonprofessional installation, although some tiles do require professional expertise. The grid formed by the placement of the tiles gives a crisp and clean appearance and enhances any interior.

Leather

Leather has always been associated with luxury and wealth. The aroma of leather is evocative of new, expensive cars and gloves and coats. Used as a tile for walls or floors, leather creates a warm and supple interior. It invites touching, and walking on leather is very tactile and satisfying. The look of leather improves with use, and

floor tiles in particularly become as inviting as an old leather chair. Leather tile comes from the sturdiest part of a bison or other cattle and is thicker than most other leathers.

QUALITIES

Leather gives an interior a sense of quality and luxury. It is available in a wide range of colors and finishes, creating subtle shadings and patterns by mixing tiles of different shades together. Leather is a natural product, and there are variations between tiles even from the same animal.

To facilitate installation, floor tiles are mounted on a wood backing with grooved joints. These tiles can also be treated to be more flame retardant.

HOW IT'S USED

Leather is used as flooring and to clad walls and other vertical surfaces. Generally, it takes about twenty-four hours for flooring tiles to set and be ready for use.

FINISHING

Wax is rubbed into the tile joints after installation, which seals and prevents moisture from creeping in. Leather floors are maintained in much the same way as hardwood.

Photo Ceramics

Digital photography has created a new genre of ceramic tile that allows the designer to create complete walls or floors using any pattern, texture, or photo desired for application to the tile. An image can be blown up and applied to a large number of tiles to create a tiled mural or scenic display. The photographic images can be manipulated to create abstract

145

patterns or realistic settings. Any image can be scanned: oil paintings, fabrics, photos, or other patterned pieces.

QUALITIES

Tiles are fired and glazed; they are as durable as any other ceramic tile and as easy to install.

All finishes are available, and price varies according to the size of installation, the type of image to be replicated, and the quantity of tiles needed.

HOW THEY'RE USED

Like any other ceramic tile, photo ceramic tiles are used throughout the home and on walls, shower enclosures, and backsplashes.

Photo ceramic tiles are used for walls, surrounds, floors, and anywhere any other tile might be used, including outdoors.

FINISHING

Once installed, no additional finish is needed. Photo ceramic tiles are cleaned the same way as any other ceramic tiles.

Pebble Tiles and Glass Tiles

Pebble and glass tiles are formed by taking the material and adhering it to a mesh background that holds the pieces in place until set on the the desired floor, wall, or surface. Pebble tiles are comprised of rounded river rocks matched for uniformity of thickness and appearance. They are used to create floors and walls that have a rustic, outdoorsy feel. Glass tiles are chosen for their vibrant color and luminous quality.

Installation with these types of scrim-mounted tiles is relatively easy and requires minimum time compared to laying individual pieces.

QUALITIES OF PEBBLE TILES

Pebble tiles are durable and hard wearing. The squares are designed to interlock for a seamless installation. There is a wide range of styles, colors, and stone types from which to choose.

HOW THEY'RE USED

Tiles are installed using an adhesive over a clean flat substrate. Smaller pebble tiles can also be curved for use around columns and rounded niches.

FINISHING

Tiles must be sealed after grouting. Cleaning is the same as most other tile installations.

QUALITIES FOR GLASS TILES

Glass tiles are available in a wide range of colors. Types of tile vary from square and rectangular to round and mosaic. They can be translucent, clear, or opalescent. Tiles are also available tumbled and frosted. They resist fading, staining, and discoloration.

HOW IT'S USED

Glass tile is best used for vertical applications in kitchens and bathrooms. They also make distinctive borders and feature tiles.

FINISHING

No additional finish is needed on tiles once installed. Clean with nonabrasive cleaners and rinse thoroughly.

PART THREE

EXCITING AND SUSTAINABLE: MODERN

The industrial revolution may have been exciting in its time, but nothing can compare to the quantum leaps we have achieved over the past fifty years. One giant leap for mankind put us on the moon, but it was the computer and our ability to rework and re-envision the materials with which we live that brought us to today's breathtaking developments in interiors. Make no mistake, the race to the moon started the process that gave us the breakthrough technology for improvements in lighting and fabric manufacturing, in addition to materials never before thought of as usable in residential or commercial interiors. Even the way professional interior designers develop plans and renderings has been impacted by the computer as a tool for productivity. Through advanced communication, technical expertise, and out-of-the-box thinking, we are beginning to see the future for the elements of interior design.

Along with the technical developments of the past fifty years, we have also become aware of our environment as a system and of the connection between the health of the planet and the actual success of mankind. We have become aware of our mortality. It comes as no surprise that the first Earth Day was celebrated around the same time we blasted our way into outer space. As we raised our eyes to the heavens, we also took a long, hard look at how we used the limited supply of materials on our own planet. Plastics were seen as one of the most egregious elements, devouring resources and becoming almost unrecyclable. Deforestation and strip mining were cited as cancers to the environment,

creating unsightly scars on the planet. We began to explore the possibilities of elements that were far easier to replace or replant.

The search for sustainable elements has brought a new energy to seemingly unremarkable woods, fabrics, and reused boards and beams. An understanding of how design elements are produced and finished helps mitigate the impact we have on the environment. Technology has helped us create plastics that are easily recycled, and new forms of lighting use far less energy than conventional bulbs. The evolution of our technological expertise will undoubtedly help us create materials that are not only cutting edge and exciting but environmentally friendly and innovative. Continued exploration of the possibilities will create new cutting-edge elements and enhance those wonderfully comforting and heartwarming elements many of us grew up with.

GLASS

Homes with full walls of glass are a relatively new concept. One hundred years ago, most glass was still handmade, and windows usually consisted of small panes separated by mullions. With the advent of modern glassmaking techniques and larger panes of glass, great expanses of glazing in homes have become commonplace and expected. With this also comes the challenge of managing heat gain and loss and the problems of glare and privacy. Double glazing—two pieces of glass separated by a vacuum—a response to the first energy crises of the early 1970s, signaled a new interest in developing ways to use glass while conserving resources and preserving privacy. As with many new innovations, double glazing was a relatively cumbersome process and was considered by some to be an inelegant solution to the problem of conservation.

The exploration of the world of reactive glass has brought a new and sleek look to windowpanes. Used at first in commercial settings for signage and displays, reactive glass quickly became a favorite of architects and professional interior designers, enhancing both exteriors and interiors across the country. The manufacturing process is generally the same for most types of glass, with small changes affecting the way the glass reacts to light or is able to manipulate light for the interior. Glare reduction and energy conservation are the most obvious applications for this type of glass, which can be expensive compared to standard glass; however, the energy savings will eventually compensate for the larger up-front cost. Although maintenance is usually the same as standard glass, installation of reactive glass requires the services of a trained professional for optimum performance.

Liquid Crystal Glazing

The value of glass has always been its transparency. But while we love bringing the outdoors in, there are times when privacy and shading are important. The use of liquid crystal glass, which becomes translucent on demand, is a solution used by architects and professional interior designers for both commercial and residential settings. The glass is composed of layers laminated together to form a solid pane, which can be single or double glazed. The inner core is a layer of liquid crystals whose inner faces have been covered with a transparent electrically conductive coating and a layer of film. This sandwich of material is then coated with glass on either side to produce the pane. The electrical coating is connected to a power source via a thin metal film on one edge of the glass. When the power is turned on the glass is clear because the crystals align to allow light through. When there is no power, the crystals are randomly spaced and create an opaque pane of glass, thus creating privacy.

QUALITIES

This glass allows virtually the same amount of light whether opaque or clear.

By programming the electric current, the panels can be used to control privacy, security, and glare at specific times of the day or night.

There is no in-between setting. The glass is either opaque or clear and uses very little energy to align the crystals.

As with other types of glass, these panes are available in various thicknesses and sizes. Panes can also be used together to create even larger expanses.

How It's Used

This glass can be used for inner applications as well as outer double glazing when the inner pane is the liquid crystal glass. For either application, it is important to use the services of a trained professional.

Finishing

There is no additional finishing required; maintain as standard glass.

SPD Glazing

Suspended particle device (SPD) glazing is a variation on the theme of liquid crystal glazing, constructed in the same general manner, which precisely controls of the amount of light allowed to pass through the glass. When the power is applied, the particles align and allow light to pass through. When the power is off, the particles diffuse, absorb the light, and the glass turns dark. With this precise control of light, the glass can play an integral part in reducing the amount of energy used to heat or cool a room. This type of glass has the potential to reduce power consumption by as much as 20 to 30 percent.

Electrochromic Glazing

This glass is, like the others, a sandwich product that uses low voltage to create the desired effect. Unlike the other two, it uses the voltage to activate a tungsten-bearing electrochromic layer that causes the color to change from clear to a darker color like blue or green.

Primarily used on exterior applications, the darkening of the glass reduces glare and reflection, which helps avoid overheating. The glass also removes the need for awnings or shades.

The coating helps keep the heat in during winter and can reduce the energy needed for air conditioning by at least half. When power is applied, the change slowly spreads from the outer edge to the whole pane of glass, and once the desired level is reached, no more power is required.

Holographic Glass

Using the same principle that creates the shimmering colors on hummingbirds and butterflies, holographic glass uses a microscopic grid to split ambient white light into its full spectrum. As you move around the glass, you will see clear glass in a rainbow of different colors or shades. The grid is sandwiched between laminated foil and clear-glass layers. One of the great

benefits is energy coneservation. On south-facing walls or roofs, holographic glass can redirect light away from the surface or redirect the light into interior rooms that might otherwise be dark.

The glass also presents decorative appeal, with a wash of rainbow shades visible as you move about the space. It is a wonderful energy saver and sends natural daylight to poorly lit areas. It can be used in all applications, including curved and shaped glass panels.

Self-Cleaning Glass

As extraordinary as it may sound, self-cleaning glass is just what the name implies. The process by which the glass becomes self-cleaning requires a specialty company and technical expertise for proper installation. Many different types of glass can be made self-cleaning. Double-pane, laminated, and thermal glass can all be coated with a thin outer layer of titanium dioxide, which will destroy organic dirt and allow it to be rinsed away in rainwater. The coating also requires daylight to activate the properties that loosen and break down organic dirt into carbon dioxide and water vapor. The coating also reduces surface tension, which allows water to simply run off the glass and not create droplets.

QUALITIES

The glass remains free of organic dirt, which saves time and money in cleaning expenses. It

Photo courtesy of Research Frontiers Inc.

also makes window cleaning much safer, especially on upper floors and sunroom roofs.

The coating will not wear away and is good for the life of the glass.

Self-cleaning glass is available in various thicknesses and different shades of clear, blue, and gray. It is about 20 percent more expensive than standard glass panes.

Sealants used should not leach silicone as it damages the coating and impairs the ability of the glass to clean itself. The glass is antibacterial and prevents fungi and mold growth. The glass cannot be etched or sandblasted.

How It's Used

Self-cleaning glass can be used for almost any external glazing requirement. The glass needs daylight and rain to work effectively, and glazed roofs should be sloped to promote water runoff. The services of a qualified professional are required to ensure proper sealants and framing patterns for optimum performance.

Finishing

Maintenance on the glass is low, but during dry periods, washing with a hose is encouraged to mimic the action of rainwater. The glass can also be cleaned with a soft cloth and soapy water.

Gloves should be worn during installation, and the glass should not be touched by uncovered fingers or hands as the oil residue could cause inorganic dirt to adhere.

Once installed, it requires several days of sunlight to activate the self-cleaning properties; the glass should not be touched during this period.

LED Tiles

Light-emitting diodes (LEDs) are not new and have been used effectively in informational signs and displays in which long-lasting bulbs are desirable. The lights are now cheaper than ever before and have become part of the interior design lexicon. Tiles are just an extension

of the use of these innovative and energy-saving lights.

Inserting small lights into tiles set in the floor or over counters as backsplashes helps accentuate architectural elements as well as give direction and promote safe movement around the house during nighttime. The lights are available in a wide range of types, colors, and styles to fit almost any design project.

Through the use of microchip computer technology, single tiles and larger installations using plastic panels can create a simple single line of lighting or shift images and patterns within a cluster of numerous diodes. Using a single color diode inset in tile creates a simple architectural line of light. With two diodes, the color can be switched between two colors. Any of the combinations can help create an environment that is both attractive and functional.

QUALITIES

The diodes give off very little heat and are long lasting. Many lights will glow for more than 80,000 hours. New generation lights are brighter and require only about three watts of electricity to operate. Installation requires a trained professional who understands the connections needed, how the cables run between the power sources, and which tiles need to be illuminated.

HOW THEY'RE USED

LED tiles are perfect for decorative and accent lighting in bathrooms, kitchens, hallways, and stairways—any place, actually, where low-level lighting can be an asset to safety.

The tiles and lighting can be used in floors, walls, and ceilings, and, when properly sealed, areas with water such as kitchens and baths.

FINISHING

There is no additional finishing needed for LED tiles, but care should be taken during installation to protect the diodes from damage or dirt.

PAPER AND TEXTILE

Nowhere else in the business of interior design do the designer, artist, scientist, and engineer work together as closely as in the world of fabrics and papers for residential use. Technology has ushered advances in ecosensitive manufacturing to rival any innovation to date. At the same time, the demands of the artist and designer have pushed engineers to create unique and industry-specific machines to produce the creations of these professionals. They have all come together in a perfect storm of creativity, expertise, and scientific advancement.

These professionals have brought us fabrics created by three-dimensional computers and sinter dust to create fabrics that require no cutting and a seamless presentation. Wall coverings that react to light and touch convey a new sense of connectivity to our environment. Fiber-optic strands have become miniscule and are woven into fabrics to create shifts in light patterns and colors. Welcome to the world of today's fabrics and papers.

Laser-Sintered Textile

The first question most of us ask is, "What is a sinter?" A sinter is a minute siliceous or calcareous deposit—in essence, silicone or calcium matter in the smallest possible form. For laser-sintered fabrics, a three-dimensional design is created in a computer. Once the design is in place, a high-powered laser fuses small particles, or sinters, into the three-dimensional design. Using a multiple-pass technique, the fabric is literally built as the layers are applied. Other material can also be used for this process. Steel and various types of plastic, such as polystyrene and nylon, have been used very successfully. The future holds almost unlimited possibilities for pattern, texture, and color when using the laser-sintered process.

QUALITIES

The fabric is a three-dimensional woven textile created without weaving, cutting, or stitching. Early prototypes resembled chain mail with a gentle feel and supple drape. Using computer-generated custom designs, the final product can incorporate variations in size, color, and pattern.

The process generates much less waste than the conventional manufacturing process.

At the moment, all laser-sintered fabrics are synthetic.

HOW IT'S USED

As the process is perfected to include more traditional looks and feels, the potential for laser-sintered fabric is as unlimited as traditional fabric.

FINISHING

No finish is required once the product is completed. Laser-sintered fabric is cared for as any other synthetic material.

Laser-Cut Fabric

Laser technology has been used for decades to create precise patterns and openings in fabrics. The process does not require building the fabric, as with the laser-sintered fabrics, but uses the simple technique of cutting patterns into fabrics. A wide range of fibers can be used for this technique, including natural weaves, cotton, and man-made materials. The results are as subtle as delicate lace and gentle contours or as bold as large open-flower patterns and geometric designs. The laser is controlled, once again, by the computer in which the design was created.

Programmable Electric Textiles

International fashion machines (IFMs) have utilized unique textile-display technology and design material to create handwoven, sensuous individual artworks, interior designs, and architectural surfaces. Their trademarked "Electric Plaid" combines woven electronic circuits, color-change inks, and drive electronics to add motion and color changing patterns to textiles and design. Programming for the fabric can create displays of changing color to make wave patterns and color changes moving from one end of the fabric to the other.

The material is created using strands of electronic yarn and hand-printed layers of color-changing ink. When activated, the changes in color occur. By connecting smaller modules of fabric together, different sizes and shapes are achieved.

QUALITIES

Active and inactive modules can be connected to create larger pieces of fabric, and color changes are programmable for varied effects. The fabric is available in many standard patterns and, of course, can be customized for an individual interior.

HOW THEY'RE USED

The panels can be hung as wall decor, panels, or fabric hangings. Programmable electric textiles can be bent and shaped in one direction.

FINISHING

No further finishing is needed for programmable electric textiles. Keep out of direct sunlight, as the inks are affected by ultraviolet (UV) light.

Electroluminescent Fabrics

Electroluminescent fabrics contain minute light sensors used to detect changes in ambient light and transfer the information to phosphorescent inks printed on the fabric. As the light changes, the image seems to either grow or fade. Like electric textiles, electroluminescent fabrics contain minute electrical wiring, the core of which is copper. Once exposed to the small electric charge, the image becomes vibrant and glowing.

By controlling the amount of electricity and light, the images printed on the fabric can either pulse across the piece or grow slowly to reveal the image.

These fabrics have been used successfully in bedding for those suffering from seasonal affective disorder by mimicking the effect of early morning light in areas of prolonged night during winter months.

There is wide potential for these fabrics for both exterior and interior furnishings.

Woven Fiber-Optical Textiles

Although fiber-optic strands have been used for decades, they are now finding their way into our homes as fabrics and accessories. Fiber optics use fine strands of acrylic or fiberglass to send light down the length of the fiber, which emerges at the end as a tiny burst of light. These strands are now tiny enough to be woven into other fabrics to create dazzling displays on pillows, cushions, and even chandeliers. Because the light source, a simple light box, can be located in a remote location without any loss of vibrancy, these types of fibers are ideal for underwater or wet areas such as kitchens and baths.

By creating small areas of abrasion on the light-transmitting fiber, the light can be splashed throughout the fabric to create an overall pattern of light and color. These fabrics resemble nothing less than a star-spangled sky when lit.

By applying different color gels to the light source with programmable color changes, the effect can combine changing colors and rhythms. The fabric should be considered delicate but has a variety of uses including drapery, slipcovers, table linen, upholstery, and lighting.

Interactive Wall Coverings

Wallpaper has also entered the arena of photoluminescence. The same techniques as those used for fabric create similar effects and can be used in numerous ways to enhance interiors. When applied to the wall, the small electric wire is embedded behind the paper. By controlling the amount of electricity through programmable transformers, the image changes with the electrical charge. The wall can glow brighter when needed and can then transform to a softer glow for evening. Once again, the possibilities are almost endless.

SUSTAINABLE

The amount of material used in the construction of a home and the finishes within the home is astounding. Homes devour huge quantities of wood, metal, concrete, glass, stone, fabrics, tiles, and assorted elements.

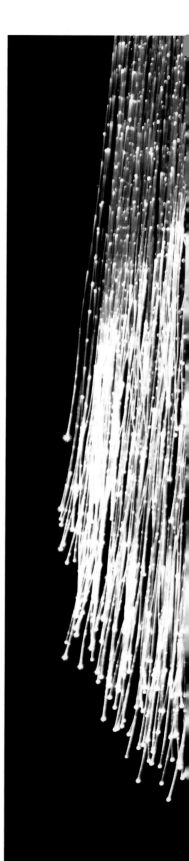

Today's design professionals make choices based not only on what is right for the job, but also what is right for the environment and the planet. Choosing sustainable materials and elements is a wise choice and one that most professionals embrace. Sustainable materials are those that, when used, do not deplete natural resources and do not damage the ecosystem. In today's vernacular, these elements are referred to as "green."

However, it is not simply a choice of bamboo over hardwood or woven sisal over a chemical-based weave. It is about where the element is grown, how much energy is used to produce it, and how far it must travel to the job site. Each step along the way increases the embodied energy within the element and the impact on our planet. Sustainable and green designs require a more diverse approach. For example, metal beams help create a home that will never need chemicals to fight pests like termites and will last far longer than one built with simple wooden studs, thus reducing the impact on the environment by reducing the energy required to rebuild the home. Materials such as concrete and stone require higher energy to produce, but when used for their high thermal mass for passive heating and cooling strategies, their embodied energy cost is balanced by far less use of energy over time to heat and cool the space. Materials that are composed of recyclable synthetics and are themselves recyclable are a great way to tackle the plastic problem. Many high-tech solutions to lighting and glass help reduce energy use and, at the same time, reduce the impact on the environment.

Deciding what materials to use and understanding how they have been produced is not an easy task. It requires an ongoing desire to educate yourself and your clients to the many options available for materials in the home. Determining one is right for the job and right for the client will be just another part of the role professional interior designers play in the new world of sustainable and green products.

Alternatives for Wood

Nothing quite matches the look and feel of a quality wood finish. Whether on flooring or a piece of furniture, wood has always been the choice for luxury and deep, splendid finishes. Used in its solid rather than composite form, wood is a good green choice. It is a renewable resource and does not require a lot in terms of chemicals and energy in the processing end of the equation. A solid wood surface or thick veneer can be sanded and refinished to give decades, if not centuries, of useful service.

But it is difficult to know for a fact where wood is grown and harvested to ensure an approved source has been used. In construction, soft woods require chemical treatments for fire retardation and to prevent pest infestation and moisture buildup, all of which impact the green value of the product.

Medium-density fiberboard (MDF), particleboard, and other composite woods use the debris and shavings cast off from solid wood production that might otherwise go to waste. These products, though, are bound together by chemicals that have an impact on human health and an adverse effect on the environment. Plywood, which uses far less formaldehyde as part of its bonding agent, is one exception.

Where, then, does that leave the professional interior designer in his or her quest for the optimum choice in green and sustainable wood products? Enter the world of wood alternatives.

Bamboo

The element produced from a mature bamboo plant has been shown to be harder than either oak or maple. Although most construction-grade bamboo comes from China and Indonesia, many of the manufacturers have taken the process of planting, harvesting, and production very seriously. They also ensure that far fewer chemicals are used (like formaldehyde in the laminating process) to guarantee an end product that is both environmentally sensitive and structurally sound. Bamboo is a grass and requires very little intervention from man during the growth process. Pesticides are not required in the growth process, and full maturity is usually reached in five to seven years. Bamboo improves poor soil, grows at an astounding rate, replenishes the atmosphere with oxygen, and is fully renewable. Although widely used as flooring,

planks, veneers, and paneling, bamboo is also used in the creation of fabrics and wallpapers.

QUALITIES

Bamboo is a plentiful, fully renewable resource. It is fast growing and reduces carbon dioxide emissions.

Strips are laminated into flooring, planks, panels, and veneers. Boards and panels are available in different widths with matching finishing details, such as molding and trim, also available.

Manufacturers have allowed the natural grain of the bamboo to come out for a variety of

interesting patterns and natural colors in finishes. Bamboo is stable and as hard as elm and oak in both flooring and paneling.

HOW IT'S USED

Flooring is by far the widest use of bamboo in today's market. Like all other hardwood flooring products, it needs to acclimate for at least seventy-two hours prior to installation. Installation is the same as for other hardwood floors.

FINISHES

Like hardwood, bamboo flooring comes prefinished and ready to use. Care of bamboo flooring is the same as hardwood flooring.

Palm

Not as readily known as bamboo, palm is an attractive alternate to hardwood for use in the home. Palm trees are grown for their nuts and fruit throughout the world on plantations, and trees that no longer produce fruit are cut down

regularly. The palm wood comes from these trees, which are about seventy-five to ninety years old and would otherwise be simply destroyed.

Palm fiber is harder on the outer edge, and it is this portion that is cut into planes, dried, and laminated with nontoxic adhesives to create the planks with which we are familiar.

QUALITIES

Palm is a renewable and abundant natural resource. The laminating process produces a durable and wood-like material. Palm is produced in the same tongue-and-groove manner as hardwood and bamboo. It comes in various graining patterns and colors.

HOW IT'S USED

Palm is used primarily for flooring. Like other flooring products, it should acclimate before installation. Palm is not suitable for wet areas. It is also available in panels and trim.

FINISHES

Like other wood flooring, palm is available finished and unfinished.

Cork

Cork as a flooring product has been in use for decades in the United States and abroad. Many of us grew up in homes with cork flooring in the kitchen.

Cork is harvested from an evergreen oak tree that sheds its bark every nine or ten years. It does not harm the tree and is completely renewable and sustainable. The cork used for flooring is actually the waste product of the cork harvested for cork bottle stoppers. Cork's cellular structure is comprised of about 90 percent

gas, which makes it lightweight, soft, and resilient. Today, cork is bound with water-based pigments that are environmentally friendly and nontoxic.

QUALITIES

Cork is a harvestable, renewable, and recyclable resource. The product is comfortable to walk on and resilient, with very good sound- and thermal-insulating properties. Cork is antibacterial, hypoallergenic, and resists mold, rot, and fire.

Cork can be brightly colored, although many flooring samples tend to be in the earth-tone family. Cork is easy to work with, and tiles can be easily replaced if damaged.

HOW IT'S USED

For interiors, cork is used primarily for flooring. It is easy underfoot and a great choice for kitchens. Cork can also be used to clad walls for a textural and dramatic design effect.

FINISHES

Sealing is necessary, although many types of cork flooring now come prefinished.

Reclaimed Wood

Wood can be reclaimed, reused, and simply refinished in so many ways that it is astounding how much product finds its way into landfills and dumps. The ease with which we can remove old barn siding and create new and interesting

interiors begs the question of why more wood isn't reused in this country. Even old ship timbers have found their way into exterior and interior applications over the years.

As is so often the case, recycling can begin in your own home. Rather than completely replacing an old wood floor, refinishing offers a wonderful chance to reuse the material and, at the same time, rethink the finish and color. It's easy to turn an old yellowish oak floor into a luxurious and inviting ebonized presentation. Kitchen cabinets can be refaced while keeping the larger and more expensive cabinet box.

When it comes to salvage wood, it is important to ensure that no pests inhabit the pieces you choose. Doors and frames, mantels, paneling,

and cabinets are all wonderful choices for reuse. There are many architectural salvage yards across America, and they often offer refinishing services, delivery, and installation. You may find hardwood pieces harder to find than softer wood pieces. Either way, there is a wealth of product to be saved.

Flooring is also easy to come by but usually requires more elaborate refinishing and reworking for use. Often nails and tacks have to be removed, but it is easy to remill the wood to fit the new space. The surfaces can be smoothed or distressed as desired. Antique flooring, particularly parquet, is harder to come by and is often very expensive.

Exterior applications also abound. Railway ties have been used for years to enhance garden spaces and terraces. Old barn siding is also a wonderful choice that offers both a unique finish and an interesting story.

Recycled Decking

In the past, decking used large amounts of hardwood and soft-wood to create the spaces most of us know and love. This had a particularly devastating impact on teak and western cedar forests. Today, however, there is an ecof-riendly alternative that creates the same look without the attendant care and maintenance needed for wood decks.

Wood polymer composites mix the waste from softwood production with recycled polyethylene waste to create decking that is, itself, recyclable.

QUALITIES

Recycled decking is totally recyclable and available in decking, posts, rails, fencing, and other exterior applications. The product resembles wood with graining features. Recycled decking is slip resistant, splinter-free, and rotproof.

HOW IT'S USED

Recycled decking can be used for all exterior applications, such as decking, garden enhancement, fencing, trellises, and edging.

FINISHING

No maintenance is required and it arrives prefinished.

ECO GLASS

Today's interiors use more glass for windows and doors than ever before. Rooms are bright and awash in sunlight. Along with this comes the added challenge of keeping rooms cool in summer and warm in winter or at night. The new generation of glass uses manufacturing techniques that incorporate a thin layer designed to bounce back heat. Called low-emissivity (low-E) glass, these panels reduce energy consumption and help keep rooms with large expanses of glass at comfortable temperatures. When incorporated as double or triple glazing, the savings can be significant.

Glass is created using very simple elements. Sand, soda, and lime are combined under high heat to create float and other glass. It is the high heat that is costly from an environmental standpoint, but glass is ecofriendly from the standpoint of recyclability. Not only can glass be remade with no loss of clarity or purity, it can also be remade into other glass products such as glass tiles and bottles.

Low-Emissivity Glass

With ordinary glass, heat is absorbed on the inner side and radiated to the cooler side; thus, heat loss. Low-E glass prevents this loss with a thin layer of metallic oxide that reflects heat back into the interior. This is the same basic principle of placing a reflective surface behind a heat source to reflect the heat back into the space.

Low-E glass was designed specifically for double glazed, not single panes of glass. Different types of coating are employed to provide high, moderate, or low solar gain. High-solar-gain glass is suitable for climates that consume the most energy heating a space, and low-solar-gain glass is more appropriate for climates using energy to cool a space. When used properly, heat loss and solar gain can be balanced in a way to keep the space at the proper temperature at all times.

QUALITIES

Low-E glass is a coated product with a microthin layer of metallic oxide. Low-E glass is virtually indistinguishable from standard glass panes. It is available in a range of dimensions.

HOW IT'S USED

Low-E glass can be used in any glazing application where heat loss or gain is an important consideration.

FINISHING

Low-E glass can be maintained as regular glass.

Recycled Plastics

Plastic is cheap, and we discard it at significant levels. It is a component of a vast range of products, including DVDs, packaging, and cell phones. From very early on, the most difficult challenge in recycling plastic has been separating the different types of polymers during the recycling process. With mandatory labeling, this has largely been rectified.

Recycled plastic has an appealing vitality in color and pattern, a by product of the manufacturing process. Random streaks and mottling imbue the product with colorful and striking features.

QUALITIES

Recycled plastic is available in boards that are one quarter to one half inch thick. The boards are worked just like wood products using saws, drills, and screws. The product is nontoxic and safe.

It should not be exposed to organic solvents or excessive heat. Colors may fade in prolonged direct sunlight.

HOW IT'S USED

Rigid sheets are used for work surfaces, shelving, cladding, furniture, and partitions. Softer, thinner sheets are used for mats, seat covers, and tablecloths.

FINISHING

Boards have either a matte or semigloss finish and may be enhanced by an application of car polish.

Wash away surface dirt with a mild detergent and warm water. Do not use abrasive cleansers or brushes, and avoid solvents such as nail polish remover.

Any small surface scratches can be removed by using fine-grade sandpaper.

TEXTILES AND PAPERS

Natural textiles and papers come from readily available, renewable, biodegradable, and recyclable sources. As such, they are a preferred choice for the ecologically minded. That said, it is important to ensure that no further chemical process was employed in the production of the material.

Many fabrics, once produced, are treated with chemicals to make them fire retardant and to reduce creasing. Not only are fabrics treated with formaldehyde as a fire retardant, but papers often have a thin layer of vinyl applied to make them water-resistant, both of which have an impact on the environment.

The type of chemical dyes and inks used for materials should also be considered. Know your source.

Synthetic backing used on fabrics can impact the overall "green" value, and natural, recyclable backings are available. Synthetic adhesives for wallpaper can be replaced by water-soluble, solvent-free adhesives.

Along with precautions concerning backing and dyes, it is also important to understand what fabrics and papers are appropriate to which application. Waste through overordering and improper use of materials is damaging to the environment and does a disservice to your client.

NATURAL FIBERS

Natural fibers all come from renewable resources and are generally processed with little energy. They have been used for centuries, and we are familiar with their characteristics. Often, though, all we think of are standbys like cotton, linen, and wool. Now is the time to think again. Sisal, coir, seagrass, and jute are also ecofriendly and readily available in today's marketplace.

Bamboo

Not only is bamboo a wonderful and sustainable flooring product, it can also be woven into soft and luxurious fabrics. The filament is round, and the fiber, when woven, is soft to the touch and inviting. Bamboo is available in chenille-like incarnations as well as flat fabrics suitable for printing. It is more affordable than cotton and uses far fewer pesticides when farmed.

Cotton

Once used primarily for clothing, cotton is now a mainstay of the residential interior design profession for its versatility and ease of coloring. Many firms around the globe are returning to the use of vegetable dyes in cotton production to reduce the impact of many chemical dyes. Unbleached, natural organic cotton has become very popular for bedding because it feels so good close to the skin.

L

la
bl

flame retardants, the more sustainable alternative is unbleached linen dyed with vegetable dyes. Linen can also be used as material for area rugs in light traffic areas.

Paper

Not only is paper superb for wall coverings, it also can be made into durable floor covering in the form of mats and area rugs. When fabricated, the paper has a crisp, clean finish that lends itself particularly well to more contemporary interior application. The paper can be dyed with both chemical and vegetable dyes and woven into many shapes and patterns.

Silk

Silk is woven from the fibers of the silkworm cocoon and is wonderfully soft and luxurious. It dyes beautifully and holds vibrant colors particularly well. Flat weaves produce material we are most used to, but silk can also be woven into thick and sumptuous fabrics of extreme beauty. Most silk is imported, which adds to its embodied cost, but it is long lasting and wonderfully adaptable.

Sisal

Sisal comes from strands harvested from the agave plant and is strong and hard wearing. Used primarily for rugs and carpeting, sisal is not water-resistant and is easily stained when wet. This same quality also makes it easy to dye, and many vibrant and colorful styles of sisal flooring are available.

Sisal can be used in many areas where wood flooring might be a choice, and it works beautifully as an underlay for area and oriental style rugs.

Wool

Wool not only comes from sheep but also from a variety of other animals, such as goats, camels, and alpacas. Wool is warm, absorbent, and naturally flame resistant. The hollow nature of the fiber also gives it great insulating properties. Natural wool products are unbleached and not treated with chemicals in any way. It does, however, dye easily and has been used for centuries for rugs and clothing. We think we know its characteristics only to discover many more attributes of this worthy fiber.

Coir, Jute, and Hemp

All of these fibers are derived from plants and processed in natural ways to create strands woven into ropes, rugs, and cloth. They are, as a group, sturdy and long lasting. Often used alone, these fibers also lend themselves to combinations with other natural fibers, particularly wool. Sisal shares this quality with this group and together they are often seen in areas of the home that require ease of maintenance and utility.

QUALITIES

These fibers can be woven into a range of weights and thicknesses. Natural fiber flooring is hypoallergenic, made from renewable resources, and biodegradable.

Most natural fiber flooring can be laid wall to wall as carpeting or made into area rugs and runners.

The pattern is most often derived from the weave employed to produce the product.

Herringbone is a popular weave and is adaptable to many interior needs.

HOW THEY'RE USED

These textiles can be used for anything in a residential setting, from window coverings and upholstery to rugs, linens, and wall coverings. Choosing a natural underlay for flooring and area rugs increases the ecofriendly footprint of these fibers.

191

FINISHING

All fibers are quite often chemically dyed and treated with chemicals to improve their fire-retardant qualities; this can reduce the overall ecocredentials. Many natural fibers stain easily, and quick cleanup is very important. Brush natural fibers regularly to prevent dirt from working into the woven material.

NATURAL PAPER

Paper recycling has been going on for generations, and today we see recycled paper in

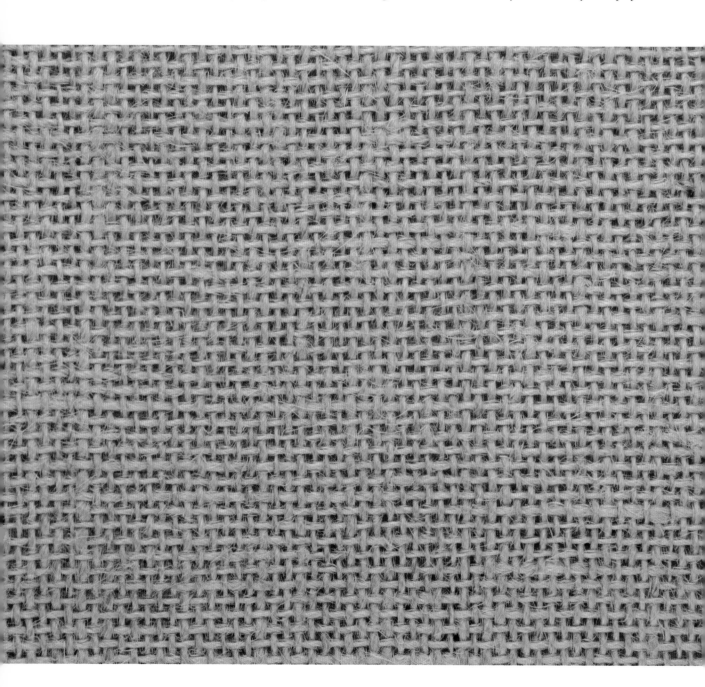

newspapers, books, magazines, paper towels, and even new wallpaper. Although it comes partially from trees, its ability to be recycled makes it an ideal choice for today's interior designs.

Like natural textiles, paper can be produced from a variety of grasses and other fibers. Machine-woven and handwoven papers are widely available and used throughout the design world to great advantage.

Bamboo

Once again, bamboo is atop the hit parade of recyclable and renewable paper sources. It is easily woven into textured paper that can resemble grass paper, and it is also made into smooth papers for walls and other applications outside the interior design industry. It dyes easily and uses strong, vibrant colors as mainstays.

Jute

Jute becomes a fine, almost silky paper when woven as wall covering and is easily dyed into soft, pale shades.

Recycled Paper

The vast majority of wallpaper today is manufactured from recycled paper. As with other applications, avoid paper with a vinyl coating to keep your choice ecofriendly.

Sisal

Sisal can be woven into wall coverings. They tend to have a fine weave and are easily dyed to create intense, vibrant colors.

Wild Grass

Used not only for standard grass paper, wild grass can often have a more pronounced reed-like quality when used on walls. It is generally

used in its natural color and form and is, therefore, low in energy consumption to produce and ecofriendly.

QUALITIES

The source for these papers is renewable, recyclable, biodegradable, and sustainable.

Natural papers help walls to breathe and help to maintain more even humidity levels. Most add remarkable depth and texture to mundane walls and interiors.

HOW IT'S USED

Natural paper is used primarily for wall coverings and to cover screens, panels, and any other vertical, flat surface. When used as wall covering, it is suggested that an ecofriendly, water-based adhesive be used.

FINISHING

There is no additional finishing required once the paper is installed. Avoid touching the paper repeatedly, and dust occasionally with a soft brush. The natural color in reeds and grasses may fade slightly when exposed to direct sunlight.

AFTERWORD

Selecting what elements to use and how to use them is the stock and trade of the professional interior designer. The challenges you face today in making these choices will impact not only the client with whom you work but also the world in which you live. This is not intended to frighten, but to instruct; it is crucial that, as a professional, you understand the materials that make up your design tool chest, as well as their sources.

I believe first and foremost that it is important to design with and invest in quality. Making choices based solely on cost usually results in designs that will not stand the test of time and ultimately will fail your client and your professional standing in the community. High quality, natural materials wear better and have already proven they can stand the test of time. The patina found on properly maintained wood flooring is almost impossible to replicate in man-made materials. Natural fibers, paper, and other materials require attention to maintain but ultimately will return the favor with long and uncomplaining service to their owners.

Recycling is far more than simply throwing a plastic bottle in the correct chute of the recycling bin. It is about choosing those products and materials that may have already been discarded. Very old building materials and furnishings have already become antiques and are, therefore, desirable in their own right. But what about those items from buildings constructed within the past twenty-five to sixty years? Is there any value there? Of course there is.

No, the word secondhand is not vulgar. Actually, secondhand may just be the most

effective form of energy conservation on the planet. The item has already acquired the embodied energy needed to produce whatever form taken. No more of that energy is required, and it has already repaid the energy cost through the first use. Now, as a secondhand item, it can be a conscientious choice and serve the environment.

Recycled bricks, pavers, glass, floors, tiles, and the myriad of other elements used in construction are available and, depending on age and quality, readily affordable. Reclaiming of extant architectural elements such as mantels, stairways, doors, and fittings is a form of secondhand acquisition. Basins, iron railings, light fixtures, and the like are also wonderful choices for new interiors.

Furniture as a secondhand element has already reached rock-star status in the form of antiques, but not all antiques need be ancient. Even those items from the mid-20th century are collectible and valuable.

Papers and fabrics are far more vulnerable to rot and decay and are not as readily found in secondhand settings. Therefore, the choice of these elements as new products is important. Both are relatively easily recycled into new elements and are good choices in themselves. But we should also consider the amount of product we consume in our interiors.

It is important to restore existing finishes and surfaces when possible. Floors can easily be sanded and refinished with little or no new material. Cabinets can be refaced. Upholstered furniture can be recovered and wood furniture refinished or repainted. Unless the interior is particularly old and outdated, it isn't necessary to rip everything out and start over. Using some existing fixtures or fittings might just give the space the warmth needed to create an inviting and interesting interior design.

As professional interior designers, we have taken on the challenge of educating ourselves about the best possible choices in materials and elements to use in our interiors. Choose elements wisely and with discretion to achieve the ultimate goals of a beautiful interior design, a happy client, and a pristine and sustainable environment.

RESOURCES

Online Sources

Allied Trade Group, Inc.
Website: www.atgstores.com

Anthropologie
Tel: (800) 543-1039
Email: service@anthropologie
.com
Website: www.anthropologie
.com

Crate & Barrel
Website: www.crateandbarrel
.com

Strauch Studio Glass
Email: strauchstudio@yahoo.com
Website: www.strauchstudio.com

Arizona (inc. Phoenix/ Scottsdale)

Facings of America
4121 North 27th Street

Phoenix, AZ 85016
Tel: (602) 955-9217
Email: info@facingsofamerica.com
Website: www.facingsofamerica
.com

Hardwoods Specialty Products
5302 West Buckeye, Bldg. A
Phoenix, AZ 85043
Tel: (602) 278-5000
Email: rgorrill@hardwoods-inc
.com
Website: www.hardwoods-inc.com

Arizona Design Center
7350 North Dobson Road
Scottsdale, AZ 85256
Website: www.arizonadesign
center.com

Facings of America
16421 North 90th Street
Scottsdale, AZ 85260
Tel: (480) 222-8480

Email: info@facingsofamerica
.com
Website: www.facingsofamerica
.com

Southern California (inc. LA area and San Diego)

Oceanside Glasstile
2293 Cosmos Court
Carlsbad, CA 92011
Tel: (760) 929-4000
Email: info@glasstile.com
Website: www.glasstile.com

Ultraglas
9200 Gazette Avenue
Chatsworth, CA 91311
Tel: (818) 772-7744
Email: sales@ultraglas.com
Website: www.ultraglas.com

Laguna Design Center
23811 Aliso Creek Road, Ste. 200
Laguna Niguel, CA 92677
Tel: (949) 643-2929
Email: lagunadc@pacbell.net
Website: www.lagunadesign
center.com

A. Rudin
8687 Melrose Avenue Ste. G172
Los Angeles, CA 90069
Tel: (310) 659-2388
Email: sales@arudin.com
Website: www.arudin.com

AAW Doors
13900 South Broadway
Los Angeles, CA 90061
Tel: (310) 516-1089
Website: www.aawdoorsinc.com

Alchemy Glass & Light, Inc.
5715 McKinley Avenue
Los Angeles, CA 90011
Tel: (323) 235-6606
Email: info@alchemyglass.com
Website: www.alchemyglass.com

Atlas Homewares
1310 Cypress Avenue
Los Angeles, CA 90065
Tel: (818) 240-3500
Email: babs@atlashomewares
.com
Website: www.atlashomewares
.com

Blue Grass Home
5818 West 3rd Street
Los Angeles, CA 90036
Tel: (323) 932-0011
Email: contact@bluegrasshome
.com
Website: www.bluegrasshome
.com

CB2
8000 W. Sunset Boulevard
Los Angeles, CA 90046
Tel: (323) 848-7111
Website: www.cb2.com

Charles Pollock Reproductions, Inc.
6824 Lexington Avenue
Los Angeles, CA 90038
Tel: (323) 962-0440
Email: info@charlespollockrepro.
com
Website: www.charlespollock
repro.com

Country Floors
8735 Melrose Avenue
Los Angeles, CA 90069
Tel: (310) 657-0510
Email: info@countryfloors.com
Website: www.countryfloors.com

DDC
8806 Beverly Boulevard
Los Angeles, CA 90048
Tel: (310) 273-5050

FabricSeen.com
11111 Santa Monica Boulevard
Los Angeles, CA 90025
Tel: (310) 479-4923
Email: anita@fabricseen.com
Website: www.fabricseen.com

Granada Tile
Los Angeles, CA 90065
Tel: (213) 482-8070
Email: info@granadatile.com
Website: www.granadatile.com

HD Buttercup
3225 Helms Avenue
Los Angeles, CA 90034
Tel: (310) 558-8900
Email: la@hdbuttercup.com
Website: www.hdbuttercup.com

Hollyhock
927 N. La Cienega Boulevard
Los Angeles, CA 90069
Tel: (310) 777-0100
Website: www.hollyhockinc.com

Kerry Joyce Textiles
2900 Rowena Avenue
Los Angeles, CA 90039
Tel: (323) 660-4442
Email: info@kerryjoycetextiles
.com
Website: www.kerryjoycetextiles
.com

L.A. Mart
1933 S. Broadway
Los Angeles, CA 90007
Tel: (800) LAMART-4
Website: www.lamart.com

Martin Pierce Hardware
5433 West Washington Boulevard
Los Angeles, CA 90016
Tel: (323) 939-5929
Email: info@martinpierce.com
Website: www.martinpierce.com

Pacific Design Center
8687 Melrose Avenue
Los Angeles, CA 90069
Email: marketing@pacificdesign
center.com
Website: www.pacificdesign
center.com

Rehab Vintage Interiors
7609 Beverly Boulevard
Los Angeles, CA 90036
Tel: (323) 668-8438
Email: info@rehabvintage.net
Website: www.rehabvintage.net

SOLI Architectural Surfaces
8483 Melrose Avenue
Los Angeles, CA 90069
Tel: (323) 951-9903
Email: info@soliusa.com
Website: www.soliusa.com

Urban Hardwoods
741 N. La Cienega Boulevard
West Hollywood, CA 90069
Tel: (424) 204-9802
Fax: (424) 204-9965
Email: la@urbanhardwoods.com
Website: www.urbanhardwoods
.com

Egg & Dart
42-829 Cook Street, Ste. 103
Palm Desert, California 92211
Tel: (760) 340-3900
Fax: (760) 340-3991
Website: www.egg-and-dart.com

Contemporary Hides
4250 C Morena Boulevard
San Diego, CA 92117
Tel: (858) 272-2025
Email: sales@contemporaryhides.
com
Website: www.contemporary
hides.com

Kravet
4090 Morena Boulevard, Ste. F
San Diego, CA 92117
Tel: (858) 273-7700
Fax: (858) 273-7764
Website: www.kravet.com

Sahara Designs
Fenton Parkway #306
San Diego, CA 92108
Tel: (858) 571-3500
Email: sales@mymoroccantile.
com, adil@saharadesigns.com
Website: www.saharadesigns.com

Eldorado Stone
1370 Grand Avenue, Bldg. B
San Marcos, CA 92078
Tel: (800) 925-1491
Email: customerservice@
eldoradostone.com
Website: www.eldoradostone.
com

Circa Furniture
655 North Robertson Boulevard
West Hollywood, CA 90069
Tel: (310) 289-6868
Email: info@phyllismorris.com
Website: www.circafurniture.com

Filmore Clark
607 North West Knoll Drive
West Hollywood, CA 90069
Tel: (310) 652-6867
Email: lee@filmoreclark.com
Website: www.filmoreclark.com

Fuse Lighting
8659 Holloway Plaza Drive
West Hollywood, CA 90069
Tel: (310) 652-2411
Email: info@fuselighting.com
Website: www.fuselighting.com

Janus et Cie
8687 Melrose Avenue, Ste. B193
West Hollywood, CA 90069
Tel: (800) 245-2687
Email: info@janusetcie.com
Website: www.janusetcie.com

Northern California (inc. San Francisco)

Sonoma Cast Stone
133A Copeland Street
Petaluma, CA 94952
Tel: (877) 939-9929
Email: steve@sonomastone.com
Website: www.sonomastone.com

Lumens Light & Living
2028 K Street
Sacramento, CA 95811
Tel: (877) 445-4486
Email: info@lumens.com
Website: www.lumens.com

A. Rudin
101 Henry Adams Street, Ste.
303
San Francisco, CA 94103
Tel: (415) 431-5021
Email: salessf@arudin.com
Website: www.arudin.com

Adeeni Design Group
PO Box 641483
San Francisco, CA 94164
Tel: (415) 928-4685
Email: info@adeenidesigngroup.
com
Website: www.adeenidesign
group.com

B. Mori & Co.
450 9th Street
San Francisco, CA 94103
Tel: (415) 431-6888
Email: info@bmori.net
Website: www.bmori.net

Bouvet Hardware
2425 3rd Street
San Francisco, CA 94107
Tel: (415) 864-0273
Email: webmaster@bouvet.com
Website: www.bouvet.com

CB2
34 Ellis Street
San Francisco, CA 94102
Tel: (415) 834-9370
Website: www.cb2.com

Conrad Imports, Inc.
600 Townsend Street, Ste. 400W
San Francisco, CA 94103
Tel: (415) 626-3303
Email: info@conradshades.com
Website: www.conradshades.com

Delinear
25 Romain Street
San Francisco, CA 94114
Tel: (415) 626-5463
Email: info@delinear.com
Website: www.delinear.com

Gump's
135 Post Street
San Francisco, CA 94108
Tel: (800)766-7628
Website: www.gumps.com

HD Buttercup
209 Townsend Street
San Francisco, CA 90291
Tel: (415) 820-4788

Email: sf@hdbuttercup.com
Website: www.hdbuttercup.com

John Whitmarsh
372 Ritch Street
San Francisco, CA 94107
Tel: (415) 652-0196
Email: info@johnwhitmarsh.com
Website: www.johnwhitmarsh.com

Lenkert Floor Coverings
2233 Alameda Street
San Francisco, CA 94103
Tel: (415) 863-0222
Email: info@lenkertfloors.com
Website: www.lenkertfloors.com

Linda Belden Handmade Rugs
550 15th Street, Ste. M-13
San Francisco, CA 94103
Tel: (415) 674-9931
Email: linda@lindabelden.com
Website: www.lindabelden.com

Luna Textiles
2415 3rd Street, Ste. 280
San Francisco, CA 94107
Tel: (415) 252-7125
Email: info@lunatextiles.com
Website: www.lunatextiles.com

McGuire Furniture
1201 Bryant Street
San Francisco, CA 94103
Tel: (415) 626-1414
Email: kendra.frisbie@kohler.com
Website: www.mcguirefurniture
    .com

Restoration Timber
111 Rhode Island Street, Ste. F
San Francisco, CA 94103
Tel: (415) 651-4276
Email: info@restorationtimber
    .com
Website: www.restorationtimber
    .com

Saint Tropez Boutique
25 Evelyn Way
San Francisco, CA 94127
Tel: (415) 702-9617
Email: sales@sainttropez
boutique.us
Website: www.sainttropez
boutique.us

Market Square (F.K.A. The San
Francisco Mart)
1355 Market Street
San Francisco, CA 94103
Website: www.sfmart.com
/FKASFMART.html

Smith & Fong Company
475 6th Street
San Francisco, CA 94103
Tel: (415) 896-0577
Email: info@plyboo.com
Website: www.plyboo.com

Soko
45 Williams Avenue
San Francisco, CA 94124
Tel: (415) 285-7656
Email: info@sokostudio.com
Website: www.sokostudio.com

Ted Boerner, Inc.
200 Lexington Street
San Francisco, CA 94107
Tel: (212) 675-5665
Email: info@tedboerner.com
Website: www.tedboerner.com

Urban Hardwoods
553 Pacific Avenue
San Francisco, CA 94133
Tel: (415) 397-9663
Fax: (415) 397-9665
Email: sf@urbanhardwoods.com
Website: www.urbanhardwoods
.com

Yangki
1026 Masonic Avenue
San Francisco, CA 94117
Tel: (415) 626-5009
Email: info@yangki.com
Website: www.yangki.com

*South Bay Design Center
7017 Realm Drive
San Jose, CA 95119
Tel: (408) 224-2620
Website: www.sbdesigncenter
.com

Chella Textiles
32 Anacapa Street
Santa Barbara, CA 93101
Tel: (805) 560-8400
Email: info@chellatextiles.com
Website: www.chellatextiles.com

Sonoma Tilemakers
7750 Bell Road
Windsor, CA 95492
Tel: (707) 837-8177
Email: marketinginfo
@sonomatilemakers.com
Website: www.sonomatilemakers
.com

Colorado

Adagio Art Glass
3910 Orchard Court
Boulder, CO 80304
Tel: (303) 905-8201
Email: rick@adagioartglass.com
Website: www.adagioartglass.
com

Parasoleil
1901 Linden Drive
Boulder, CO 80304
Tel: (303) 589-4524
Email: hello@parasoleil.com
Website: www.parasoleil.com

Aceray, LLC
104 Broadway, Ste. 200
Denver, CO 80203
Tel: (303) 733-3404
Email: info@aceray.com
Website: www.aceray.com

Denver Design Center
595 South Broadway
Denver, CO 80209
Tel: (303) 733-2455
Email: ddc@denverdesign.com
Website: www.denverdesign.com

Denver Merchandise Mart
451 E. 58th Avenue, # 470
Denver, CO 80216
Email: info@denvermart.com
Website: www.denvermart.com

Egg & Dart
595 South Broadway, Ste. 110
East
Denver, Colorado 80209
Tel: (303) 744-1676
Fax: (303) 744-6742
Website: www.egg-and-dart.com

Emuamericas LLC
104 Broadway, Ste. 500
Denver, CO 80203
Tel: (800) 726-0368
Email: info@emuamericas.com
Website: www.emuamericas.com

Lee Jofa
595 South Broadway, Ste. 101E
Denver, CO 80209
Tel: (303) 733-3470
Fax: (303) 733-3457
Website: www.leejofa.com

Mattei Glass Studio
303 South Broadway, Ste.
   200-514
Denver, CO 80209
Tel: (303) 292-0441
Email: mmattei@mcleodusa.net

Vitraform
3500 Blake Street
Denver, CO 80205
Tel: (303) 295-1010
Email: inquiries@vitraform.com
Website: www.vitraform.com

Wm Ohs, Inc.
5095 Peoria Street
Denver, CO 80239
Tel: (303) 371-6550
Email: bill@williamohsdesign.com
Website: www.wmohs.com

Connecticut

Old Wood Workshop
193 Hampton Road
Pomfret Center, CT 06259
Tel: (860) 655-5259
Email: info@oldwoodworkshop
   .com
Website: www.oldwoodwork
   shop.com

Design Source CT
1429 Park Street, Ste. 100
Hartford, CT 06106
Tel: (860) 951-3145
Email: info@designsourcect.com
Website: www.designsourcect.com

Design Within Reach
700 Canal Street, 3rd Floor
Stamford, CT 06902
Tel: (800) 944-2233
Website: www.dwr.com

Kravet/Lee Jofa
360 Fairfield Avenue
Stamford, CT 06902
Tel: (203) 504-2640
Fax: (203) 504-2638
Website: www.kravet.com and
   www.leejofa.com

Rosemary Hallgarten
993 Post Road East
Westport, CT 06880
Tel: (203) 259-1003
Email: info@rosemaryhallgarten
   .com
Website: www.rosemaryhall
   garten.com

Florida (North, inc. Tampa and Orlando)

*Designers' Workshop
2618 University Boulevard West
Jacksonville, FL 32217
Tel: (904) 731-4494
Fax: (904) 730-3178
Email: info@designerswork
   shopjax.com
Website: www.designerswork
   shopjax.com

Trinity Tile Group
115 SW 49th Avenue Ste. 105
Ocala, FL 34474
Tel: (352) 369-0444
Email: info@trinitytile.com
Website: www.trinitytile.com

*Interiors Trading Company, Inc.
408 Virginia Drive
Orlando, FL 32803
Tel: (407) 228-9966
Fax: (407) 228-9977
Email: info@orlandoitc.com
Website: www.floridafabric.com

*Interiors Trading Company, Inc.
315 North Willow Avenue
Tampa, FL 33606
Tel: (813) 258-6678 or (800)
   330-6678
Fax: (813) 258-6738
Email: info@tampaitc.com
Website: www.floridafabric.com

Florida (South, inc. Miami)

Capitol Lighting
7301 North Federal Hwy.
Boca Raton, FL 33487
Tel: (561) 994-9570
Email: info@1800lighting.com
Website: www.1800lighting.com

Design Center of the Americas
1855 Griffin Road
Dania Beach, FL 33004
Tel: (954) 920-7997
Website: www.dcota.com

Miromar Design Center
10800 Corkscrew Road, Ste. 382
Estero, Florida 33928
Tel: (239) 390-5111
Fax: (239) 390-8211
Website: www.miromardesign
   center.com

Carl's Furniture Showrooms, Inc.
5051 N. University Drive
Fort Lauderdale, FL 33321
Email: info@carls.com
Website: www.carls.com

Old Florida Lumber Company
25 SE 25th Street
Fort Lauderdale, FL 33316
Tel: (954) 760-5800
Email: info@oldfloridalumber
   .com
Website: www.oldfloridalumber
   .com

Unique Wholesale Distributors, Inc.
6811 N.W. 15th Avenue
Fort Lauderdale, FL 33309
Tel: (800) 824-1277
Fax: (954) 975-0297
Website: www.uniquewholesale
   .net

Deco Design
7400 NW 55th Street
Miami, FL 33166
Tel: (305) 597-4747
Email: info@decodesigncenter.com
Website: www.decodesigncenter
   .com

Élitis
6073 NW 167th Street, Ste. C-8
Miami, FL 33015
Tel: (800) 916-2036
Email: contact.usa@elitis.fr
Website: www.elitis.fr

Glass and Glass
601 NW 11th Street
Miami, FL 33136
Tel: (305) 416-5001
Email: info@glassandglass.com
Website: www.glassandglass.com

Green America Décor
1 NE 40th Street, Ste. 2
Miami, FL 33137
Tel: (888) 600-0473
Email: info@greenamericadecor
   .com
Website: www.greenamerica
   decor.com

Jessie D'Angelo Studio, Inc.
15420 SW 82nd Court
Miami, FL 33157
Tel: (786) 242-7055
Email: info@jessiedangelo.com
Website: www.jessiedangelo.com

Keys Granite, Inc.
8788 NW 27th Street
Miami, FL 33172
Tel: (305) 477-7363
Email: sales@keysgranite.com
Website: www.keysgranite.com

Luminaire
8950 NW 33rd Street
Miami, FL 33172
Tel: (305) 437-7975
Email: info@luminaire.com
Website: www.luminaire.com

Opustone Granite & Marble
   Distributors
3200 NW 77th Court
Miami, FL 33122
Tel: (305) 594-4200
Email: sales@opustone.com
Website: www.opustone.com

PSCBATH
7179 NW 52nd Street
Miami, FL 33166
Tel: (305) 594-7120
Email: info@pscbath.com
Website: www.pscbath.com

Raleo
Interlink 1238 Box 669435
Miami, FL 33166
Tel: (800) 697-1880
Email: design@raleo.com
Website: www.raleo.com

Space Lighting
282 NW 25th Street
Miami, FL 33127
Tel: (305) 373-4422
Email: info@spacelighting.com
Website: www.spacelighting.com

Travertine Mart
940 Lincoln Road, Ste. 207
Miami Beach, FL 33139
Tel: (305) 763-8682
Email: contact@travertinemart
   .com
Website: www.travertinemart.com

CB2
1661 Jefferson Ave
Lincoln Road Mall
Miami Beach, FL 33139
Tel: (305) 672-5155
Website: www.cb2.com

Georgia (inc. Atlanta)

Amba
1294 Logan Circle
Atlanta, GA 30318
Tel: (404) 350-9738
Email: info@ambaproducts.com
Website: www.ambaproducts.com

Americas Mart
240 Peachtree Street NW, Ste.
   2200
Atlanta, GA 30303
Tel: (404) 220-3000
Website: www.americasmart.com

Amtico International Inc.
66 Perimeter Center East, 7th
   Floor, Ste. 700
Atlanta, GA 30346
Tel: (404) 267-1907
Website: www.amtico.com

Antiques & Interiors of Sandy
   Springs
6336 Roswell Road NE
Atlanta, GA 30328
Tel: (404) 250-1057
Email: aiss@bellsouth.net
Website: www.aiss-online.com

Architectural Accents
2711 Piedmont Road NE
Atlanta, GA 30305
Tel: (404) 266-8700
Email: info@architecturalaccents
.com
Website: www.architectural
accents.com

*Atlanta Decorative Arts Center
351 Peachtree Hills Avenue NE,
Ste. 138
Atlanta, GA 30305
Tel: (404) 812-6995
Website: www.adacatlanta.com

Belvedere
721 Miami Circle NE, Suite 105
Atlanta, GA 30324
Tel: (404) 352-1942
Email: belvedere@mindspring
.com
Website: www.belvedereinc.com

BoBo Intriguing Objects
1194 Logan Court NW
Atlanta, GA 30318
Tel: (404) 355-2309
Email: info@bobointringuing
objects.com
Website: www.bobointriguing
objects.com

CB2
1080 Peachtree Street NE
Atlanta, GA 30309
Tel: (404) 894-3763
Website: www.cb2.com

Currey & Company
50 Best Friend Road
Atlanta, GA 30340
Tel: (678) 533-1500
Email: info@curreyco.com
Website: www.curreycodealers
.com

Dedar
1694 Chantilly Drive
Atlanta, GA 30324
Tel: (404) 325-2726
Email: roger@dedar-usa.com
Website: www.dedar.com

Domus, Inc.
1919 Piedmont Road
Atlanta, GA 30324
Tel: (404) 872-1050
Email: sales@domusinternational
.com
Website: www.domusinternational
.com

Francois & Co.
1990 Defoor Avenue
Atlanta, GA 30318
Tel: (404) 355-2589
Email: info@francoisandco.com
Website: www.francoisandco.com

Global Weave
451-B Bishop Street
Atlanta, GA 30318
Tel: (678) 999-7501
Email: info@global-weave.com
Website: www.global-weave.com

Jerry Pair
351 Peachtree Hills Avenue NE,
Ste. 508
Atlanta, GA 30305
Tel: (404) 261-6337
Email: info@jerrypair.com
Website: www.jerrypair.com

Jim Thompson
1694 Chantilly Drive
Atlanta, GA 30324
Tel: (404) 325-5004
Email: info@jimthompson
thaisilk.com
Website: www.jimthompson
fabrics.com

Olde Savannah Flooring, Inc.
4750 Bakers Ferry Road
Atlanta, GA 30336
Tel: (404) 691-3834
Email: customercare@olde
savannahflooring.com
Website: www.olde
savannahflooring.com

Mannington Commercial
1844 U.S. Hwy. 41 SE
Calhoun, GA 30703-7004
Tel: (800) 241-2262
Email: lisa_mccoy@mannington
.com
Website: www.mannington.com

Shaw Contract Group
410 Old Mill Road
Cartersville, GA 30120
Tel: (877) 502-7429
Email: shawcontractgroup
@shawinc.com
Website: www.shawcontract
group.com

Clayton Miller
2304 Dalton Industrial Court
Dalton, GA 30721
Tel: (706) 281-4501
Email: sales@clayton-miller.com
Website: www.clayton-miller.com

Stone Connection
3045 Business Park Drive
Norcross, GA 30071
Tel: (770) 662-0188
Email: usinfo@stoneconnection
.com
Website: www.stoneconnection
.com

Illinois (inc. Chicago area)

Lee Jofa
3441 North Ridge Avenue
Arlington Heights, IL 60004
Tel: (847) 394-4364
Fax: (847) 394-3757
Website: www.leejofa.com

Red Rock Tile Works
1550 North 5th Street
Charleston, IL 61920
Tel: (217) 345-2300
Email: sales@redrocktileworks
.com
Website: www.redrocktileworks
.com

A. Rudin
200 World Trade Center, Ste.
1711
Chicago, IL 60654
Tel: (312) 494-9300
Email: saleschi@arudin.com
Website: www.arudin.com

Antonio Lupi Chicago
516 North Wells Street
Chicago, IL 60610
Tel: (312) 329-1550
Email: info@antoniolupichicago
.com
Website: www.antoniolupi
chicago.com

Baker
222 Merchandise Mart Plaza, Ste.
1414
Chicago, IL 60654
Tel: (312) 329-9410
Website: www.bakerfurniture.com

CB2
800 W. North Avenue
Chicago, IL 60642
Tel: (312) 787-8329
Website: www.cb2.com

Elements
741 North Wells Street
Chicago, IL 60654
Tel: (877) 642-6574
Website: www.elementschicago
.com

Holly Hunt, Ltd.
801 West Adams, Ste. 700
Chicago, IL 60607
Tel: (312) 329-5999
Email: info@hollyhunt.com
Website: www.hollyhunt.com

Hydrology
435 North LaSalle Street
Chicago, IL 60654
Tel: (312) 832-9000
Email: us@hydrologychicago.com
Website: www.hydrologychicago
.com

Lacava
6630 West Wrightwood Avenue
Chicago, IL 60707
Tel: (773) 637-9600
Email: info@lacava.com
Website: www.lacava.com

Merchandise Mart
222 Merchandise Mart Plaza
Chicago, IL 60654
Tel: (312) 527-4141
Website: www.mmart.com
/mmart

Mico Designs, Ltd.
1432 West 21st Street
Chicago, IL 60608
Tel: (312) 243-0770
Email: info@micodesigns.com
Website: www.micodesigns.com

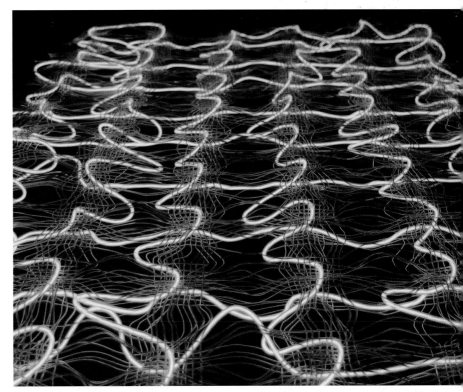

Photo courtesy of Neil Musson, Mackay Design Studio (www.mackaydesignstudio.co.uk).

Rode Bros.
300 West Grand Avenue
Chicago, IL 60654
Tel: (773) 398-8758
Email: aaronl@rodebros.com
Website: www.rodebrothers.com

Sietto
2730 North Greenview Avenue,
   Ste. J
Chicago, IL 60614
Tel: (312) 513-6968
Email: andrew@sietto.com
Website: www.sietto.com

Stewart Floor
156 West Superior Street, Ste.
   201
Chicago, IL 60654
Tel: (312) 265-5434
Email: sean@stewartfloor.com
Website: www.stewartfloor.com

StonePeak Ceramics
314 West Superior Street
Chicago, IL 60654
Tel: (312) 506-2800
Email: info@stonepeakceramics
   .com
Website: www.stonepeak
   ceramics.com

Indiana

The Trade Source
Indiana Design Center
200 South Rangeline Road, Ste.
   226
Carmel, IN 46032
Tel: (317) 818-8250
Email: info@thetradesource.net
Website: www.thetradesource.net

Massachusetts (inc. Boston area)

Artaic—Innovative Mosaic
21 Drydock Avenue, 7th Floor
Boston, MA 02210
Tel: (617) 418-1928
Email: info@artaic.com
Website: www.artaic.com

Boston Design Center
One Design Center Place
Boston, MA 02210
Tel: (617) 449-5506
Email: info@bostondesign.com
Website: www.bostondesign.com

FilzFelt
300 A Street
Boston, MA 02210
Tel: (617) 391-6230
Email: info@filzfelt.com
Website: www.filzfelt.com

Kravet (Showroom)
One Design Center Place, Ste. 126
Boston, MA 02210
Tel: (617) 338-4615
Fax: (617) 439-6006
Website: www.kravet.com

Landry & Arcari Oriental Rugs
   and Carpeting
333 Stuart Street
Boston, MA 02116
Tel: (617) 399-6500
Email: diodice@landryandarcari
   .com
Website: www.landryarcari.com

Mosaic Loft
21 Drydock Avenue
Boston, MA 02210
Email: info@mosaicloft.com
Website: www.mosaicloft.com

Michigan

Israel's Windows, Floors, and More
2340 28th Street SE
Grand Rapids, MI 49508
Tel: (616) 247-0290 or (888)
   247-0290
Fax: (616) 247-0292
Email: wfm@israels.com
Website: www.windowsfloorsand
   more.com

Lee Jofa
1700 Stutz Drive, Ste. 105
Troy, MI 48084
Tel: (248) 649-3020
Fax: (248) 649-3512
Website: www.leejofa.com

Michigan Design Center
1700 Stutz Drive, Ste. 25
Troy, MI 48048
Tel: (877) 393-0330
Website: www.michigandesign
   .com

Minnesota

Hirshfield's
950 Prairie Center Drive
Eden Prairie, Minnesota 55344
Tel: (952) 996-0644
Website: www.hirshfields.com

Hirshfield's
325 East Lake Street
Minneapolis, Minnesota 55408
Tel: (612) 823-7209
Website: www.hirshfields.com

International Market Square
275 Market Street
Minneapolis, MN 55405
Tel: (612) 338-6250
Website: www.imsdesigncenter
   .com

Hirshfield's
420 Crossroads Drive SW
Rochester, Minnesota 55902
Tel: (507) 285-9594
Website: www.hirshfields.com

Stone Holding Co.
633 Prosper Drive
Waite Park, MN 56387
Tel: (320) 251-1540
Email: info@stoneholding.com
Website: www.stoneholding.com

Hirshfield's
2024 South Robert Street
West St. Paul, Minnesota 55118
Tel: (651) 451-4046
Website: www.hirshfields.com

Missouri

Interior Design Center of St.
  Louis
11610-11660 Page Service Drive
St. Louis, MO 63146
Tel: (314) 983-0218
Website: www.idcstl.com

New Jersey

BoConcept
20 Pulaski Street
Bayonne, NJ 07002
Tel: (201) 433-4461
Email: boconcept@boconcept
  -usa.com
Website: www.boconcept.us

New Jersey Decorating Exchange
3 New Bridge Road
River Edge, NJ 07661
Tel: (201) 342-0110
Website: www.decoratingx.com

New York (Upstate)

Kravet
1685 Elmwood Avenue
Buffalo, NY 14207
Tel: (716) 874-1737
Fax: (716) 874-5084
Email: interiordesignresources
  @gmail.com
Website: www.kravet.com

Frederick William
9521 Steuben Valley Road
Holland Patent, NY 13354
Tel: (315) 865-8670
Email: frederick@frederick
  william.com
Website: www.frederickwilliam
  .com

Antique & Vintage Woods of
  America
2290 Route 199
Pine Plains, NY 12567
Tel: (518) 398-0049
Email: info@antiqueandvintage
  woods.com
Website: www.antiqueandvintage
  woods.com

**New York (City and
  surrounding area)**

Kravet, Inc.
225 Central Avenue South
Bethpage, NY 11714
Tel: (516) 293-2000 or (800)
  645-9068
Fax: (516) 293-2737
Email: customer.service@kravet
  .com
Website: www.kravet.com

Cosmopolitan Glass
1668 61st Street
Brooklyn, NY 11204
Tel: (718) 837-7711
Email: sales@cosmopolitanglass
  .com
Website: www.cosmopolitanglass
  .com

Watermark
350 Dewitt Avenue
Brooklyn, NY 11207
Tel: (718) 257-2800
Email: info@watermark-designs
  .com
Website: www.watermark
  -designs.com

David Goldberg Design Co.
23-23 Borden Avenue, 2nd Floor
Long Island City, NY 11101
Tel: (718) 361-8181
Email: info@davidgoldberg
  design.com
Website: www.davidgoldberg
  design.com

MechoShade Systems
42-03 35th Street
Long Island City, NY 11101
Tel: (718) 729-2020
Email: info@mechoshade.com
Website: www.mechoshade
  systems.com

A. Rudin
979 Third Avenue, Ste. 1201
New York, NY 10022
Tel: (212) 644-3766
Email: salesny@arudin.com
Website: www.arudin.com

ABC Home
881/888 Broadway
New York, NY 10003
Tel: (212) 473-3000
Email: ruginfo@abchome.com
Website: www.abchome.com

Aero
419 Broome Street
New York, NY 10013
Tel: (212) 966-1500
Website: www.aerostudios.com

AFNY
22 West 21st Street, 5th Floor
New York, NY 10010
Tel: (212) 243-5400
Email: info@afnewyork.com
Website: www.afnewyork.com

Ankasa Accessories
135 E 65th Street
New York, NY 10021
Tel: (212) 861-6800
Email: info@ankasa.com
Website: www.sachinandbabi.com

Apartment 48
115 W 16th Street
New York, NY 10011-5766
Tel: (212) 807-1391
Website: www.apartment48.com

Architects & Designers Building
150 East 58th Street
New York, NY 10155
Tel: (212) 644-2766
Email: lfoa@mmart.com
Website: www.adbuilding.com

Architectural Systems, Inc.
150 West 25th Street, 8th Floor
New York, NY 10001
Tel: (212) 206-1730
Email: sales@archsystems.com
Website: www.archsystems.com

Area, Inc.
58 East 11th Street
New York, NY 10003
Tel: (212) 924-7084
Email: sales@area-inc.net
Website: www.areahome.com

Artistic Tile, Inc.
38 West 21st Street
New York, NY 10010
Tel: (877) 237-4097
Email: moreinfo@artistictile.com
Website: www.artistictile.com

Aster Cucine
325 West 16th Street
New York, NY 10011
Tel: (877) 890-3800
Email: info@astercucineusa.com
Website: www.astercucineusa.
   com

Baccarat
625 Madison Avenue, 2nd Floor
New York, NY 10022
Tel: (212) 826-4130
Email: wendy.horton@baccarat.fr
Website: www.baccarat-us.com

Bart Halpern
136 West 21st Street, 11th Floor
New York, NY 10011
Tel: (212) 414-2727
Email: info@barthalpern.com
Website: www.barthalpern.com

Bazzeo/NYLOFT Kitchens &
   Home Interiors
6 West 20th Street
New York, NY 10011
Tel: (212) 206-7400
Email: info@bazzeo.com
Website: www.bazzeo.com

Bleu Nature
605 Third Avenue, 24th Floor
New York, NY 10158
Tel: (212) 370-4408
Email: gpervilhac@edgemarkets
   .com
Website: www.bleunature.com

Bruno Triplet
118 Spring Street, 3rd Floor
New York, NY 10012
Tel: (212) 966-733
Email: info@brunotriplet.com,
   newyork@brunotriplet.com
Website: www.brunotriplet.com

Callidus Guild Wall Covering
20 Lexington Avenue
New York, NY 11238
Tel: (718) 783-0329
Email: studio@callidusguild.com
Website: www.callidusguild.com

Carini Lang
335 Greenwich Street
New York, NY 10013
Tel: (646) 613-0497
Email: info@carinilang.com
Website: www.carinilang.com

Carleton V, Ltd.
979 Third Avenue, 15th Floor
New York, NY 10022
Tel: (212) 355-4525
Email: info@carletonvltd.com
Website: www.carletonvltd.com

CassaDecor
295 5th Avenue, Ste. 111
New York, NY 10016
Tel: (877) 258-5177
Email: info@cassadecor.com
Website: www.cassadecor.com

CB2
451 Broadway
New York, NY 10013
Tel: (212) 219-1454
Website: www.cb2.com

Complete Tile Collection
42 West 15th Street
New York, NY 10011
Tel: (212) 255-4450
Email: denes@completetile.com
Website: www.completetile.com

Cowtan & Tout
111 Eighth Avenue, Ste. 930
New York, NY 10011
Tel: (212) 647-6900
Email: miry_park@cowtan.com
Website: www.cowtan.com

Davis and Warshow
A & D Building
150 East 58th Street, 4th Floor
New York, NY 10155
Tel: (212) 688-5990
Email: showrooms@dwny.com
Website: www.daviswarshow.com

Decoration & Design Building
979 3rd Avenue
New York, NY 10022
Tel: (212) 759-5408
Fax: (212) 751-8130
Website: www.ddbuilding.com

DDC
136 Madison Avenue
New York, NY 10016
Tel: (212) 685-0800
Email: sales@ddcnyc.com
Website: www.ddcnyc.com

Diane Paparo Studio
20 West 22nd Street, Ste. 1516
New York, NY 10010
Tel: (212) 308-8390
Email: design@paparo.com
Website: www.dpstudiousa.com
    /home.html

Dransfield & Ross
54 West 21st Street
New York, NY 10010
Tel: (212) 741-7278
Email: dandr44@aol.com
Website: www.dransfieldandross
    .biz

Ebony and Co. Flooring
156 Fifth Avenue, Ste. 707
New York, NY 10010
Tel: (646) 786-0330
Email: newyork@ebonyandco
    .com
Website: www.ebonyandco.com

F. Schumacher and Co.
79 Madison Avenue
New York, NY 10016
Tel: (212) 213-7900 or (800)
    523-1200
Email: info@fsco.com
Website: www.fschumacher.com

Fabricteria Maki
4877 Broadway, Ste. 41
New York, NY 10034
Tel: (212) 304-0540
Email: info@fabricteriamaki.com
Website: www.fabricteriamaki
    .com

First Editions Wallcoverings &
    Fabrics, Inc.
979 Third Avenue Concourse
    Level
New York, NY 10022
Tel: (212) 355-1150
Email: shellyn@firsteditions.com
Website: www.firsteditions.com

Flair
88 Grand Street
New York, NY 10013
Tel: (212) 274-1750
Email: info@flairhomecollection
    .com
Website: www.flairhomecollection
    .com

George Smith LLC
315 Hudson Street
New York, NY 10013
Tel: (212) 226-4747
Email: nyshowroom@george
    smith.com
Website: www.georgesmith.com

Gracious Home
1220 Third Avenue
New York, NY 10021
Tel: (212) 517-6300
Email: info@gracioushome.com
Website: www.gracioushome.com

Groundplans
136 East 56th Street
New York, NY 10022
Tel: (212) 888-9366
Email: jharrow@groundplans.com
Website: www.groundplans.com

H. Theophile
136 West 21st Street, 11th Floor
New York, NY 10011
Tel: (212) 727-0074
Email: sales@htheophile.com,
    studio@htheophile.com
Website: www.htheophile.com

Howard Kaplan Designs
240 East 60th Street
New York, NY 10022
Tel: (646) 443-7170
Email: hkaplandesigns@aol.com
Website: www.howardkaplan
    designs.com

Innovations in Wallcoverings, Inc.
150 Varick Street, 9th Floor
New York, NY 10013
Tel: (212) 807-6300
Email: customerservice
@innovationsusa.com
Website: www.innovationsusa
.com

Jed Johnson Home
32 Sixth Avenue
New York, NY 10013
Tel: (212) 707-8989
Email: info@jedjohnson.com
Website: www.jedjohnson.com

Kravet
200 Lexington Avenue, 4th Floor
New York, NY 10016
Tel: (212) 725-0340
Fax: (212) 684-7350
Website: www.kravet.com

Liora Manne
210 11th Avenue, 7th Floor
New York, NY 10001
Tel: (212) 989-2732
Email: info@lioramanne.com
Website: www.lioramanne.com

Lori Weitzner
54 West 21st Street, Ste. 404
New York, NY 10010
Tel: (212) 414-1089
Email: info@loriweitzner.com
Website: www.loriweitzner.com

LV Wood
24 West 20th Street
New York, NY 10011
Tel: (212) 627-9663
Email: info@lvwoodfloors.com
Website: www.lvwoodfloors.com

Maharam
251 Park Avenue South
New York, NY 10010
Tel: (800) 645-3943
Email: clientservices@maharam
.com
Website: www.maharam.com

Manhattan Cabinetry
227 East 59th Street
New York, NY 10022
Tel: (212) 750-9800
Email: 59th@manhattancabinetry
.com
Website: www.manhattan
cabinetry.com

Mi Casa Collection
445 West 37th Street, Ste. 2FW
New York, NY 10018
Tel: (646) 688-5615
Email: info@micasacollection.com
Website: www.micasacollection
.com

Nemo Tile
48 East 21st Street
New York, NY 10029
Tel: (212) 505-0009
Email: nemo@nemotile.com
Website: www.nemotile.com

NY Stone Manhattan
30 West 21st Street, Ground
Floor
New York, NY 10010
Tel: (212) 256-1500
Email: info@nystonemanhattan
.com
Website: www.nystonemanhattan
.com

OdeGard
200 Lexington Avenue, Ste. 1206
New York, NY 10016
Tel: (212) 545-0069
Email: info@odegardinc.com
Website: www.odegardinc.com

Paris Ceramics
D & D Building
150 East 58th Street, 7th Floor
New York, NY 10155
Tel: (212) 644-2782
Website: www.parisceramics.com

Pollack Textiles
150 Varick Street
New York, NY 10013
Tel: (212) 627-7766
Website: www.pollackassociates
.com

Robin Reigi
48 West 21st Street, Ste. 1002
New York, NY 10010
Tel: (212) 924-5558
Email: info@robin-reigi.com
Website: www.robin-reigi.com

Rug Art
979 Third Avenue, Ste. 1518
New York, NY 10022
Tel: (212) 207-8211
Email: vidal@rug-art.net
Website: www.rug-art.net

SA Baxter
200 Lexington Avenue, Ste. 716
New York, NY 10016
Tel: (800) 407-4295
Website: www.sabaxter.com

Samuel Heath
111 East 39th Street, Ste. 2R
New York, NY 10016
Tel: (212) 599-5177
Email: info@samuel-heath.com
Website: www.samuel-heath.com

Sherle Wagner, International
300 East 62nd Street
New York, NY 10065
Tel: (212) 758-3300

Email: custserv@sherlewagner
.com
Website: www.sherlewagner.com

Simon's Hardware and Bath
421 Third Avenue
New York, NY 10016
Tel: (212) 532-9220
Email: info@simonshardwareand
bath.com
Website: www.simonshardware
andbath.com

Stone Source
215 Park Avenue South
New York, NY 10003
Tel: (212) 979-6400
Email: info@stonesource.com
Website: www.stonesource.com

Studium, Inc.
150 East 58th Street, 7th Floor
New York, NY 10155
Tel: (212) 486-1811
Email: info@studiumnyc.com
Website: www.studiumnyc.com

Sun Décor Fabrics
200 Lexington Avenue, Ste. 417A
New York, NY 10016
Tel: (212) 213-2703
Email: info@sundecorfabrics.com
Website: www.sundecorfabrics
.com

Walters Wicker, Inc.
979 Third Avenue
New York, NY 10022
Tel: (212) 758-0472
Email: info@walterswicker.com
Website: www.walterswicker.com

Wood Essentials
PO Box 843 Lenox Hill Station
New York, NY 10021
Tel: (212) 717-1112

Email: mail@woodessentials.com
Website: www.woodessentials.com

Hudson Valley Lighting
106 Pierces Road
PO Box 7459
Newburgh, NY 12550
Tel: (845) 561-0300
Website: www.hudsonvalley
lighting.com

Nevada

Las Vegas Market
495 S. Grand Central Parkway,
Ste. 2203
Las Vegas, NV 89106
Tel: (888) 962-7469
Website: www.lvdesigncenter.com

North Carolina

Century Furniture
PO Box 608
Hickory, NC 28603
Tel: (828) 328-1851
Website: www.centuryfurniture
.com

*A. Hoke, Ltd.
725 South Cedar Street
Charlotte, NC 28202
Tel: (704) 358-0277
Website: www.ahokelimited.com

*Karen Saks
2116 Hawkins Street
Charlotte, NC 28203
Tel: (704) 377-9277
Website: www.karensaks.com

*A. Hoke, Ltd.
1405 Capital Boulevard
Raleigh, NC 27603
Tel: (919) 832-5555
Website: www.ahokelimited.com

*Karen Saks
1508 Capital Boulevard
Raleigh, NC 27603
Website: www.karensaks.com

North Dakota

Hirshfield's Paints & Coatings
3552 East Divide Avenue
Bismarck, ND 58501
Tel: (701) 751-2090 or (877)
    868-6276
Website: www.hirshfields.com

Hirshfield's ICI
3223 Main Avenue
Fargo, ND 58103
Tel: (701) 235-0549
Website: www.hirshfields.com

Ohio

Ohio Design Centre
23533 Mercantile Road
Beachwood, OH 44122
Tel: (216) 831-1245
Website: www.ohiodesigncentre
    .com

Cellura Designs, Inc.
5040 Richmond Road
Cleveland, OH 44146
Tel: (216) 464-6600 or (888)
    889-1992
Fax: (216) 464-3076
Email: celluradesigns@cellura
    designs.com
Website: www.celluradesigns
    .com

Ballard Designs
5568 West Chester Road
West Chester, OH 45069
Tel: (800) 536-7551
Email: customerservice@ballard
    designs.net
Website: www.ballarddesigns.com

Oregon (Portland area)

Ann Saks
8120 NE 33rd Drive
Portland, OR 97211-2018
Tel: (503) 281-7751
Email: web.feedback@kohler.com
Website: www.annsaks.com

Kravet
1800 NW 16th Avenue, Ste. 100
Portland, OR 97209
Tel: (503) 228-4040
Fax: (503) 228-5247
Website: www.kravet.com

Pratt & Larson Ceramics
1201 SE Third Avenue
Portland, OR 97214
Tel: (503) 231-9464
Email: marketing@prattand
    larson.com
Website: www.prattandlarson.com

Pennsylvania (Philadelphia)

Galbraith & Paul
116 Shurs Lane
Philadelphia, PA 19127
Tel: (215) 508-0800
Email: info@galbraithandpaul.com
Website: www.galbraithandpaul
    .com

Marketplace Design Center
2400 Market Street
Philadelphia, PA 19103
Tel: (215) 561-5000
Website: www.marketplacedc.com

*Design Trade
2837 Smallman Street
Pittsburgh, PA 15222
Tel: (412) 281-6415
Fax : (412) 281-6412
Website: www.designtrademkt
    .com

Tennessee

Eykon Wallcovering Source
5675 East Shelby Drive
Memphis, TN 38141
Tel: (901) 365-1903
Email: info@eykon.net
Website: www.eykon.net

Seabrook Wallcoverings, Inc.
1325 Farmville Road
Memphis, TN 38122
Tel: (901) 320-3500
Email: web.service@seabrk.com
Website: www.seabrookwallpaper
    .com

Mission Stone & Tile Co.
2930 Sidco Drive
Nashville, TN 37204
Tel: (615) 244-6448
Email: info@missionstonetile.com
Website: www.missionstonetile
    .com

Texas (North inc. Dallas)

Arteriors Home
4430 Simonton Road
Dallas, TX 75244
Tel: (877) 488-8866
Email: sales@arteriorshome.com
Website: www.arteriorshome.com

Campbell Contract
PO Box 561483
Dallas, TX 75356
Tel: (214) 631-4242
Email: sales@campbellcontract
    .com
Website: www.campbellcontract
    .com

*Dallas Design Center
1250 Slocum Street
Dallas, TX 75207
Tel: (214) 698-1300
Website: www.designcenterdallas
.com

Dallas Market Center
2100 Stemmons Freeway
Dallas, TX 75207
Tel: (214) 655-6100 or (800)
DAL-MKTS
Website: www.dallasmarket
center.com

Daltile
7834 C.F. Hawn Fwy.
Dallas, TX 75217
Tel: (214) 398-1411
Website: www.daltile.com

Joseph Noble
2025 Irving Boulevard, Ste. 110
Dallas, TX 75207
Tel: (214) 741-8100
Email: info@josephnoble.com
Website: www.josephnoble.com

Levantina USA, Inc.
11180 Zodiac Lane
Dallas, TX 75229
Tel: (214) 736-9875
Email: commercial@levantinausa
.com
Website: www.levantina.com

Link
13766 Beta Road
Dallas, TX 75244
Tel: (972) 385-7380
Email: efreeland@linkdesign
solutions.com
Website: www.linkdesign
solutions.com

Minolochi
1316 Slocum Street
Dallas, TX 75207
Tel: (241) 748-1800
Email: inquiry@minolochi.com
Website: www.minolochi.com

Perennials
140 Regal Row
Dallas, TX 75247
Tel: (214) 638-4162
Email: info@perennialsfabrics
.com
Website: www.perennialsfabrics
.com

Source One Wallcovering
11123 Shady Trail
Dallas, TX 75229
Tel: (866) 862-4316
Email: info@sourceonewall
covering.com
Website: www.sourceonewall
covering.com

TRI-KES
11123 Shady Trail
Dallas, TX 75229
Tel: (972) 484-8120
Fax: (972) 484-8190
Email: samples@tri-kes.com
Website: www.tri-kes.com

Veneerstone
1720 Couch Drive
McKinney, TX 75069
Tel: (214) 491-5100
Fax: (972) 767-3909
Email: david.andrews
@tejasstone.com
Website: www.veneerstone.biz

Texas (South inc. Austin and
Houston)

Seasonal Living
211 East Alpine Road
Austin, TX 78704
Tel: (512) 554-5738
Email: sales@seasonalliving.com
Website: www.seasonalliving.com

Mod Green Pod
1507 West Koenig Lane
Austin, TX 78756
Tel: (512) 524-5196
Email: info@modgreenpod.com
Website: www.modgreenpod.com

Decorative Center of Houston
5120 Woodway Drive
Houston, TX 77056
Tel: (713) 961-9292
Website: www.decorativecenter
.com

Hokanson
5120 Woodway Drive, Ste. 190
Houston, TX 77056
Tel: (800) 255-5720
Email: sales@hokansoncarpet.com
Website: www.hokansoncarpet
.com

OKITE Quartz Surfacing
Northwoods Industrial Park
12227 FM 529, Ste. K
Houston, TX 77041
Tel: (713) 849-3800
Fax: (713) 849-3835
Email: info@okite.us
Website: www.okite.us

Motif Modern Living
5 Brent Boulevard, Ste. 100
Kyle, TX 78640
Tel: (512) 262-2211
Email: info@motiffurniture.com
Website: www.motiffurniture.com

Lucifer Lighting Company
3750 IH35 North
San Antonio, TX 78219
Tel: (210) 227-7329
Email: b.west@luciferlighting
    .com
Website: www.luciferlighting
    .com

Virginia

*Designer's Market
2107 North Hamilton Street
Richmond, VA 23230
Tel: (804) 353-5224
Email: info@designers-market.com
Website: www.designers-market
    .com

Washington D.C.

The Washington Design Center
300 D Street SW
Washington, DC 20024
Tel: (202) 646-6100
Fax: (202) 488-3711
Website: www.dcdesigncenter
    .com

Washington (inc. Seattle)

Artisan Crafted Lighting
PO Box 1030
Langley, WA 98260
Tel: (360) 321-2636
Fax: (360) 321-2585
Email: info@artisancrafted.com
Website: www.artisancrafted
    lighting.com

Alchemy Collections
2029 Second Avenue
Seattle, WA 98121
Tel: (206) 448-3309
Email: info@alchemycollections
    .com
Website: www.alchemycollections
    .com

Christian Grevstad Collection,
    Ltd.
PO Box 46048
Seattle, WA 98146
Tel: (206) 938-4360
Email: info@grevstad.com
Website: www.christiangrevstad
    collection.com

Flopping Fish Productions
900 First Avenue South, #307
Seattle, WA 98134
Tel: (206) 624-5122
Email: lisa@floppingfish.com
Website: www.floppingfish.com

Jeffrey Braun Furniture
416 McGraw Street
Seattle, WA 98109
Tel: (888) 866-4011
Fax: (888) 866-4587
Email: lnb@jeffreybraun.com
Website: www.jeffreybraun.com

Seattle Design Center
 5701 Sixth Avenue South
Seattle, WA 98108
Tel: (866) 776-0095
Email: sdcinfo@hines.com
Website: www.seattledesign
    center.com

Steam Escapes
2232 B 1st Avenue South
Seattle, WA 98134
Tel: (206) 321-5064
Fax: (206) 624-0471
Email: info@steamescapes.com
Website: www.steamescapes.com

Urban Hardwoods
2101 First Avenue
Seattle, WA 98121
Tel: (206) 443-8099
Fax: (206) 443-8862
Email: sea@urbanhardwoods.com
Website: www.urbanhardwoods
    .com

Viola Park
997 Western Avenue
Seattle, WA 98104
Tel: (206) 467-5524
Email: seattle@violapark.com
Website: www.violapark.com

INDEX

acrylic, 55, 123, 127–128, 166
adhesive, 24, 39, 45, 49, 54, 88,
    149, 173, 182, 200
aggregate, 87, 92–93
antibacterial, 22, 45, 128, 142,
    161, 176
antimicrobial, 92
antique flooring, 178
antistatic, 45, 142
backsplash, 14, 22, 25, 31, 40,
    88, 92, 117, 123, 138, 149,
    163
bamboo, 168–171
    flooring, 171
    natural fiber, 183
    natural paper, 194
    rugs, 58
biodegradable, 182, 191, 200
    not biodegradable, 49
brick, 26–31
    brick paver, 29
    cladding, 17, 19–20, 92, 107,
        123, 138–140, 181

honeycombed, 29
kiln, 31, 39
lightweight, 29
mortar, 31, 88, 91
standard construction, 29
vitrified brick, 30
weathered, 29
wire-cut, 29
burn-resistant, 45
carpet, 49–57
    acrylic, 55
    backings, 53
    Brussels weave, 55
    cord, 55
    densities, 53
    flat weave, 54, 63, 187
    fries-cut pile, 55
    loop pile, 55
    nonwoven carpet, 54
    nylon, 54
    pile constructions, 53
    polyester, 54
    polypropylene, 54

shag pile, 55
shag-style carpet, 54
simple cut pile, 55
stain-resistant, 55
tufted carpet, 54–55
velvet-cut pile, 55
viscose, 55
wool, 53-55
wool-blend, 53
woven carpet, 54–55
carving, 88
cement, 84, 87, 88, 92, 93
    gravel, 84, 87
    Portland cement, 84
ceramic, 26–43
    non-porcelain ceramic, 39
    photo ceramics, 145–149
    porcelain ceramic, 39
chemical-resistant, 88
chemical treatments, 168
chrome, 83
classic, 2, 5, 7, 49, 64
clay, 27, 31, 33, 39

commercial, 4–5, 77, 79, 93, 151, 154, 156
composite stones, 128, 132
composite woods, 168
concrete, 5, 83–95
    advanced cast, 92–93
    cast on-site, 87–88
    precast, 87–88
    translucent, 87, 91–92
Corian®, 128
cork, 175–176
cost-effective, 22, 49
decorative laminate, 132–138
digital photography, 145
double-glazing, 84, 153, 158
ecofriendly, 2, 179–180, 183, 191, 197, 200
edging, 14, 88, 179
epoxy resin, 88
etching, 88
fabrics, 1, 5, 53, 84, 127, 148, 152, 164–166, 170, 187, 203
    acetate, 67, 69
    acrylic fabrics, 128
    bedspreads, 69, 71
    brocade, 67
    canvas, 69
    chintz, 69
    comforters, 71
    creasing, 70, 182
    curtains, 65, 69
    cushions, 71, 166
    damask, 69
    dupion, 69
    flax, 70, 185
    gingham, 69
    lace, 69–70
    linen, 64, 67, 69, 70, 71, 166, 183, 185–186
    machine-washable, 67
    moire, 70
    muslin, 70
    pillows, 71, 166
    silk taffeta, 71

table linen, 71, 166
tweed, 71
velvet, 71
fibers, 1, 54–55, 58, 62, 67–78
    absorbent, 185, 189
    bleached, 185
    chemically dyed, 182, 184, 185, 192
    coir, 183, 190
    hemp, 190–192
    jute, 43, 55, 77, 183, 190–192
    seagrass, 183
    silkworm, 187
    sisal, 168, 189
        agave plant, 189
        natural fiber, 183
        paper, 189–190
        recycled, 198
    unbleached, 184–185, 189
    vegetable dyes, 184–185, 187
    wild grass, 198–200
fireproof, 87
fire-retardant, 65, 182, 192
fissure, 15
flame-resistant, 189
flame-retardant, 145, 185
formaldehyde, 168–169, 182
Formica®, 135
glass
    acid-etched, 117
    acrylic mirror, 123
    alcoves, 123
    colored glass, 93, 117
    decorative glass, 84, 117–120
    electrochromic glazing, 159
    energy conservation, 154, 203
    float glass, 112
    frameless mirror, 123
    glare reduction, 154
    glass blocks, 120
    glass tiles, 149–150, 180
    glazing, 112, 153, 161, 180
    heated mirrors, 123
    high-solar-gain glass, 180
    holographic glass, 159–160

honeycombed glass, 114
laminated glass, 114, 117
liquid crystal glazing, 156–158
low-emissivity (low-E) glass, 180
low-solar-gain glass, 180
mirror, 120–126
mirror tile, 123
mirrored furniture, 123
opaque glass, 117
reactive glass, 154
safety glass, 117
screen-printed glass, 117
self-cleaning glass, 160–161
shatterproof, 123
SPD glazing, 158–159
strengthened glass, 114–116
tempered glass, 114
textured glass, 117
thermal glass, 160
titanium dioxide, 160
wired glass, 114
glue, 7, 22, 31, 54, 111
grass paper, 194, 198
grit, 26, 31, 39, 58
grouting, 19, 26, 88, 150
handmade, 24, 27, 29, 31, 54, 62, 69, 91, 93, 112, 153
heat-resistant, 92, 132
herringbone, 30, 45, 191
honed, 13–14, 17, 19–20, 41, 88
hygienic, 96, 138
hypoallergenic, 45, 128, 176, 191
industrial, 4–5, 79, 88, 96, 111
insect-resistant, 87
insulation, 29, 87–88
leather, 142–145
light
    diodes, 161–164
    "Electric Plaid," 165
    electroluminescent fabrics, 165
    fiber-optic strands, 164, 166
    International Fashion Machines, 165

laser-sintered textiles, 164
LED tiles, 161–164
light sensors, 165
photoluminescence, 166
polystyrene, 164
sinter dust, 164
linoleum, 43–48
linseed oil, 31, 35, 43
machine-made, 29, 31, 54,
    62–63, 69
maintenance-free, 30, 49
man-made, 1, 22, 53, 62, 67, 69,
    71, 127, 141, 165, 201
matte, 20, 55, 181
medium-density fiberboard
    (MDF), 168
metal
    aluminum, 96, 107, 111, 114,
        117
    anodized aluminum, 111
    heat-tempered aluminum, 111
    base, 96, 103
    brass, 93
    bronze, 1
    chromium, 105
    conduct electricity, 101
    copper, 1, 101, 165
    corrode, 101
    corrugated, 104
    gold, 101
    iron, 96, 101–104, 203
        cast iron, 101
        corrugated iron, 103
        iron ore, 101
        iron oxide, 101
        pig iron, 101
        smelt, 101
        wrought iron, 101–103
    lead, 96
    metal ores, 1
    nickel, 105
    noble, 101
    platinum, 101
    precious, 83
    rust, 96, 101, 104, 107

    sheet, 103
    silver, 101
    steel, 96, 101–110, 164
        carbon steel, 105
        stainless steel, 83, 96,
          105–110
    tarnish, 101
    tin, 1, 112
    tungsten, 107
metal fabrics, 84
moisture-resistant, 65, 132
molding, 170
molds, 88, 101
mottling, 20, 180
nonmagnetic, 111
nonporous, 22, 128
nonslip, 20, 58, 88, 93, 117, 142
non-toxic, 128, 173, 176, 181
palm, 171–174
paper
    American roll, 77
    block-printed papers, 77
    burlap, 77
    double-width papers, 77
    European roll, 77
    grass cloth, 77
    hand-printed papers, 77
    handwoven paper, 193–194
    machine-printed paper, 74
    machine-woven paper, 193
    natural fiber papers, 77
    photogravure, 74
    rotor press, 74
    screen-printed paper, 74
    silk-screen technique, 74
    untrimmed, 74, 77
    wallpaper, 64, 71–78, 166,
        170, 182, 193, 197
particleboard, 168
pebbles, 142
pebble tiles, 149
petroleum product, 49
pesticides, 169, 183
pest-resistant, 96
photoceramics, 84

pine resin, 43
plasterboard, 39
plastic, 114, 117, 127, 151–152,
    163–164, 168, 180–181, 201
plywood, 168
polyester, 54, 71
porous, 20, 29, 31, 88, 111
powdered cork, 43
powdered limestone, 43
pre-finished, 171, 176, 179
printing, 49, 64, 71, 74, 183
recycled, 5, 101, 127, 152, 203;
    see also sustainable.
    bricks, 203
    decking, 179
    plastics, 180–181
    paper, 192–193, 197
resin, 19, 22, 43, 88, 93, 128,
    132, 138–141
ribbed, 88, 114
rubber, 141–142
    rubber floors, 84
rugs, 58–64
    bamboo, 58
    Bokhara, 63
    Caucasian, 63
    Chinese, 62
    contemporary rugs, 64
    cotton, 58, 63–64
    craft rugs, 64
    dhurries, 63
    flokati, 64
    kelims, 63
    Persian, 58–62
    serape rugs, 64
    shag pile, 64
    silk, 58, 62, 64
    Tibetan, 62
    Turkish, 63
    Turkoman, 63
    wool, 58, 62–64
sand, 20, 24, 84, 87, 88, 92, 180
sandblasting, 20, 114
sheet resin, 138–141
shell, 88

slip-resistant, 29, 179
solar heating, 9, 84
solid composite materials, 128
stain-resistant, 22, 55
stone, 1, 9–27, 40–41, 49, 83,
       87–88, 166, 168
  calcite, 19
  engineered stone, 22–26
  feldspar, 13, 39
  floors, 26, 58, 93
  granite, 11, 13–14
  igneous rock, 10–11, 20
  limestone, 19–20
  marble, 7,   11, 14–17, 93
  metamorphic rocks, 11, 17
  mica, 13, 17
  quartz, 13, 20, 22, 128–132
  sandstone, 20–22
  sedimentary stone, 11–13,
     19–20
  shale, 17
  slate, 11, 17–19
  travertine, 19
structural supports, 87
sustainable, 2, 152, 168–169,
     175, 183, 185, 200,
     204
  salvage, 13, 177–178
  salvage yards, 178
  secondhand, 5, 201, 203
  reclaimed, 5
     brick, 29
     stone, 13
     tiles, 31–33
     warehouses, 103
     wood, 176–178
  recyclable synthetics, 168
  refinishing, 177–178
synthetic, 48, 127–142, 164,
    168, 182
terrazzo, 93–95
  precast, 93
thermoplastic, 48, 127, 135
tiled mural, 145
tiles

artisan-made, 31
ceramic, 35–39
  floors, 24, 145
  mosaic, 29, 40–43
     ceramic, 40
     composite, 40
     earthen, 40
     glass, 40
     stone, 40–41
  quarry, 33–35
  terra-cotta, 27–29, 31–33
traction, 20
trim, 170, 173
tumbled, 17, 20, 24, 29, 31, 41,
  150
tungsten, 107, 159
underfloor heating, 9, 87, 142
upholstery, 64, 70–71, 166, 191
veneer, 168, 170
vinyl, 48–49, 64, 117, 182, 197
  "off-gas," 49
  polyvinylchloride (PVC), 48–49
  roll form, 49
viscose, 55, 69
warping, 49
waterproof, 17, 29, 39, 49
water-resistant, 39, 45, 49, 182,
  189
weather-proofed, 107
weather-resistant, 88
wood
  hardwood, 58, 145, 168, 171,
     173, 178–179
  rot-proof, 179
  softwood, 179
  splinter-free, 179
  wood flour, 43
  wood polymer composites, 179
wool, 183, 189
  carpet, 53–55
  fabric, 64, 67, 69, 71
  rug, 58, 62–64
zinc, 93, 104, 107
Zodiaq®, 128

NOTES

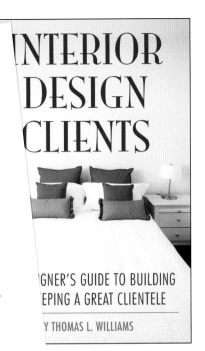

INTERIOR
DESIGN
CLIENTS

IGNER'S GUIDE TO BUILDING
EPING A GREAT CLIENTELE

Y THOMAS L. WILLIAMS

Keeping a Great Clientele

n, and a sound understanding of how to manage those cli-
mative yet fun read for entrepreneurial designers interested
and manage their clientele. Thomas L. Williams, designer,
hallenges that can waylay even seasoned designers.

can often be intimidated by interior designers and can some-
of the process. This unreasonable intimidation can hinder the designer-client relation-
ship and can even stop clients from asking for what they really want. As a result the designer could fail to
satisfy the client and have them walk away with a negative impression of the designer's work.

Learning why clients fear their interior designer and developing strategies to allay those fears is essential for
gaining and keeping a satisfied clientele. Everything from good client, project, and time management to interview techniques and staff and paperwork organization can contribute to a highly rewarding working relation-
ship and are important aspects of the business rarely addressed by the interior design community as a whole.
Interior Design Clients covers the subjects rarely taught in design schools, such as specific presentation and
interview skills and how to sell to the market.

Green Interior Design

Lori Dennis

Paperback
$24.95

Award-winning designer and author Lori Dennis proves interior design can be both stylish and environmentally sustainable in this easy-to-use, entertaining guide. Dennis discusses every aspect of interior design—furniture and accessories, window treatments, fabrics, surface materials, appliances, plants, and more—from a green perspective in terms of reducing waste and pollution and turning a home into a healthy, comfortable environment. Readers will learn how to:

- use sustainable materials like bamboo, cork, and recycled glass to enhance interiors
- search thrift shops and antique stores for vintage hidden treasures
- find the best vendors for purchasing green products
- use plants and locally cut flowers to improve indoor air quality and brighten up rooms
- replace lawns with indigenous plants and edible gardens
- keep rooms clean with effective and nontoxic products
- use energy-efficient lighting and maximize natural light
- apply for different types of green certification

Packed with over 100 color photographs, lists of the best green vendors, and profiles of leading green designers, this book is a thorough guide for anyone who wants to create beautiful interiors while decreasing the waste and pollution generated by the building industry.

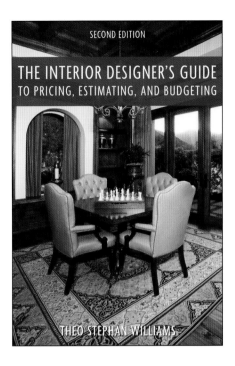

The Interior Designer's Guide to Pricing, Estimating, and Budgeting, Second Edition

Theo Stephan Williams

Paperback
$24.95

Empowered by the step-by-step guidance in this book, interior designers will be able to establish prices and budgets that make their clients happy and their businesses profitable. This second edition is updated throughout and includes additional material on time management and numerous interviews with leading designers. Written by a designer and veteran expert on pricing, estimating, and budgeting systems, *The Interior Designer's Guide to Pricing, Estimating, and Budgeting* provides practical guidelines on how to value the cost of designing commercial or residential interiors, from the designer's creative input to the pricing of decorating products and procedures.

This book shows how to determine a profitable and fair hourly rate, balance the client's budget with his or her wishes and needs, negotiate prices with suppliers and contractors, write realistic estimates and clear proposals, manage budgets for projects of all sizes and types, and position the firm's brand in relation to its practices. Interviews with experienced interior designers, case studies, and sidebars highlight professional pitfalls and how to master them, from daily crisis management and self-organization to finding the perfect office manager. This superbly thorough guide offers pricing, estimating, and budgeting advice that is a necessity for every designer and firm pushing to bolster the bottom line.

Interior Design Clients: The Designer's Guide to Building and Keeping a Great Clientele
by *Thomas L. Williams* (6 x 9, 234 pages, paperback, $24.95)

Green Interior Design
by *Lori Dennis* (8 ½ x 10, 160 pages, paperback, $24.95)

The Interior Designer's Guide to Praicing, Estimating, and Budgeting, Second Edition
by *Theo Stephan Williams* (6 x 9, 208 pages, paperback, $24.95)

Starting Your Career as an Interior Designer
by *Robert K. Hale and Thomas L. Williams* (6 x 9, 240 pages, paperback, $19.95)

Interior Design Practice
by *Cindy Coleman* (6 x 9, 256 pages, paperback, $24.95)

Marketing Interior Design
by *Lloyd Princeton* (6 x 9, 224 pages, paperback, $24.95)

Business and Legal Forms for Interior Designers
by *Tad Crawford and Eva Doman Bruck* (8 ½ x 11, 208 pages, paperback, $29.95)

How to Start and Operate Your Own Design Firm: A Guide for Interior Designers and Architects
by *Albert W. Rubeling* (6 x 9, 256 pages, paperback, $24.95)

The Challenge of Interior Design: Professional Values and Opportunities
by *Mary V. Knackstedt* (6 x 9, 256 pages, paperback, $24.95)

How to Start a Faux Painting or Mural Business, Second Edition
by *Rebecca Pittman* (6 x 9, 240 pages, paperback, $24.95)

Brand Thinking and Other Noble Pursuits
by *Debbie Millman* (6 x 9, 256 pages, hardcover, $29.95)

To see our complete catalog or to order online, please visit *www.allworth.com*.